Structured Programming with COBOL Examples

Structured Programming with COBOL Examples

Earl H. Parsons Jr.

Writer's Showcase
New York Lincoln Shanghai

Structured Programming with COBOL Examples

Writer's Showcase
an imprint of iUniverse, Inc.

For information address:
iUniverse
2021 Pine Lake Road, Suite 100
Lincoln, NE 68512
www.iuniverse.com

ISBN: 0-595-25094-7 (Pbk)
ISBN: 0-595-65034-1 (Cloth)

Printed in the United States of America

I would like to dedicate this book to my wife, Lynn, for her patience with this hobby of writing books.

Other Books by the Author:

Mr. Parsons is also the author of the text The Database Expert's Guide to IDEAL, which was published by McGraw Hill in 1989. IDEAL is a trademark of Computer Associates Inc.

Contents

List of Figures

Preface

Thank you for picking up this book. Writing a book is difficult, but it is worth the effort if someone reads what you have to say.

If you are looking for a book on COBOL syntax, I am afraid that you have the wrong book. The purpose of this book is to define what structured programming is, and how its principals can be applied to building structured programs. The final conclusion is that by using structured programming we can use a single base line program, and then trade out modules to give each unique program it's specific functionality.

We will use COBOL for our examples for a number of reasons. First, the people who will read this book will know COBOL, or will at least know enough to be able to follow the examples. It is very difficult trying to discuss programming if both sides don't understand the language in which the examples are written.

The second reason is that, with over 20 years of professional experience, the author understands COBOL, and with this experience will (hopefully) be able to avoid embarrassing syntax errors in the examples. Programs can be compiled and tested, but books cannot.

The third reason is that COBOL is still the most widely used business language. Part of the user communities' disappointment with the Information Systems community stems from our inability to produce reliable and flexible computer systems. The main reason for this is our inability (unwillingness?) to discipline ourselves to write structured COBOL programs. Hopefully, this book will help us find a way to do a better job.

The fourth reason is that members of the academic community have been deriding COBOL for years, saying that COBOL is a poor language, and that it cannot be structured. Personally, I like a good challenge. I use to jump out of perfectly good airplanes, and starting to write a new book is a very similar experience.

We will begin our discussion by defining structured programming, and we will review and explain the development of the principles of structured programming. In the second chapter we will discuss the process of parsing a human defined task into manageable units of work.

In the third chapter we will introduce the concepts of coupling and cohesion, which we can use to judge the "structure" of a program. In the fourth chapter we will use these concepts to review the overall structure of the basic COBOL program. In the fifth chapter we will use coupling and cohesion to organize our working storage.

In the sixth chapter we will use coupling and cohesion to build a basic COBOL program. It is our contention that there is really only one basic COBOL program, and that any application problem can be solved by adding or deleting modules from this basic model program.

Chapters 7, 8, and 9 are devoted to proving this contention. We will add modules to the basic program so that we can produce multiple reports, produce multiple outputs, load and validate data against an internal program table, process with an internal sort, validate data against an external database, use report breaks, and process a two file merge. Chapters 10 and 11 will be used to show how our basic program structure into a CICS program. Chapter 12 contains a discuss on the building of subroutines.

In chapter 13 we will conclude our discussion by identifying why the GO TO and the GO TO EXIT verbs are not acceptable in structured programming.

Those who care about such things may notice that I often use the pronoun "he" throughout the text, instead of "she", or "they" or what ever happens to be politically correct these days. Please do not accuse me of any kind of gender bias. It simply is a matter of key strokes, and the fact that after all of these years I still only use two fingers when I type.

I hope that you find this book helpful in your work.

Chapter 1

What is Structured Programming

Computer programming is the process of translating a computer user's needs into a set of instructions that the machine can execute. There are four characteristics of a good program.

The first characteristic of a good program is that it must be effective. The program must work correctly, be reliable and provide accurate and consistent output. It must be easy for the user to understand and operate, and it must fulfill a valid need.

The second characteristic of a good program is that it must be available on time. The quarterly Sales Tax report must run at the end of the quarter. W2 forms must be produced by the end of January. The author knows of one large retailer who pegged their future on a new purchasing and inventory control system. The system failed and the firm went under.

The third characteristic of a good program is adaptability. Business changes on a daily basis. As companies struggle for profits, or even survival, management tends to try any reasonable (and sometimes unreasonable) idea. Yesterday's truth that was written in stone can be blowing sand tomorrow. The author worked on a telephone call billing system where the format of the vendor's input file changed twice in a year. And then there was the sales tax computation module of a billing / invoicing system which seemed to require a change from some state every week.

The fourth characteristic of a good program is that it must be efficient. The author worked at a client site which had an accounting accruals system that ran for 14 hours. This inefficiency caused the users to have to make manual adjustments for any problems that were encountered because they could not afford to rerun the process. Restructuring the process reduced the run time to less than an hour.

The problem is that humans and machines do not think the same way. Humans see a solution in the form of a grand design, with infinite, complicated variables, many of which can be simply ignored. Computers think in binary; yes or no; true or false; black or white. Every variable that the human can think of must be translated into machine instructions. Every possible event must be accounted for.

The author developed a system to compute long distance call charges. In the final walkthru, the user asked if we had included the special calculations for calls to the Caribbean area codes. "You didn't tell me about any special charges on calls to the Caribbean." I countered. The user replied that I didn't ask. I then asked if there were special charges on calls to Pennsylvania.

A human's solution can ignore problems based on a low probability of occurrence. But the function of a computer system is very closely associated with Murphy's Law "Everything that can go wrong will." The author had a professor who wrote a program which had a piece of logic which would never be executed. At the end of this logic he had the program write a line which stated "You can't get here!". He submitted the program one afternoon and went home. The program produced three boxes of paper with the single spaced line "You can't get here!" before it was finally cancelled. Thinking they could not get any deeper in trouble than they already were for canceling the professor's job, the operators debated the ramifications of wrapping the boxes in Christmas ribbon. Discretion, and thoughts of upcoming final exams, prevailed. But copies of the last numbered page circulated through the department for several weeks.

An example of the difference between human and machine thinking can be seen in the classic problem of building a peanut butter sandwich. In human thinking, this is a fairly simple task, which we can break down to subordinate tasks:

1) Get the bread.
2) Get the peanut butter.
3) Get the jelly.
4) Get a knife.
5) Put the peanut butter on the bread.
6) Put the jelly on the bread.
7) Put the two pieces of bread together.

There are two kinds of knowledge, tacit and explicit. (Afuah 38) Knowledge is explicit if it can be codified, spelled out in drawings, verbalized, or programmed. Some of this knowledge is learned from observation, like the fact that the sides of the bread with the peanut butter and the jelly go together. Tacit knowledge cannot be codified or programmed. Some of this knowledge comes instinctively, like going to mom if the jelly jar is empty. Humans have the ability to develop tacit knowledge without related explicit knowledge. This is demonstrated by the ability of a child prodigy to play the piano, or the ability of a baby to respond to the sound of its mother's voice, or the ability of a student in a physics class to derive one equation from two other equations.

Computers do not have the capability to develop tacit knowledge. They can only work with explicit knowledge. The solution of each variable must be defined before the entire problem can be solved. This must be done by supplying instruction as either a series of decision statements (IF-THEN-ELSE, GO TO, PERFORM, ADD), or as a series of data arrays (a table containing a list of acceptable state code abbreviations). We must tell the computer which two sides of the sandwich go together, and what to do if there is no more jelly. We must tell the computer how to play the piano or how to derive the equation. We must then find a process where we can collect these variables and their answers, so that we organize what we want the computer to learn. This is like developing a lesson plan to teach a elementary school class.

The organization and design of this process was originally done with flow charts. Flow charts were developed to show the flow of processing control through a program. The chart would show the order of processing, the effect that decisions have on program processing, and the timing of the loop processing control. The problem with flow charts is best described by Lem O. Ejiogu in his book Effective Structured Programming.

"Flowcharts begin somewhere: then branch left and right, up and down, from page to page, back again, then off again, repetitiously, on and on. There is a general loss of control. The entry and exit points are almost unrecognizable. For large systems the maze is almost endless. Trying to trace the flow of a data name is like looking for a needle in a haystack. Trying to trace backwards for the source of a data item is like labeling the sources of a drop of water at a river confluence." (Ejiogu page 4)

These shortcomings became more acute as the machines and the problems that they were called on to solve became more and more complicated. The flowcharts became more complicated, and the programs that were written from them became almost impossible to manage and maintain.

The art of programming then began a movement toward the concept of "structured programming." The most critical concepts of this movement can be found in a number of academic papers. The most important of these papers are:

Böhm, C. and Jacopini, G. "Flow Diagrams, Turning Machines and Languages With Only Two Formation Rules." Communications of the ACM: Vol. 9, #5 (1966); pp. 366-371.

Dijkstra, E.W. "Go To Statement Considered Harmful."
Communications of the ACM: Vol. 11. #3 (1968), pp. 147-148.

Dijkstra, E.W. "The Humble Programmer."
Communications of the ACM: Vol. 15. #10 (1972), pp. 859-866.

Endres, Albert "An Analysis of Errors and Their Causes in System Programs."
IEEE Transactions on Software Engineering: Vol. SE-1. #2 (1975), pp. 140-149.

Mills, Harlan D. "The New Math of Computer Programming."
Communications of the ACM: Vol. 18. #1 (1975), pp. 43-48.

Wirth, Niklaus "Program Development by Stepwise Refinement."
Communications of the ACM: Vol. 14. #4 (1971), pp. 221-227.

Wirth, Niklaus "On the Composition of Well-Structured Programs"
Computing Surveys: Vol. 6. #4 (1974), pp. 247-249.

In these papers, the authors laid down some important principles. The first principle is that there is a limit to how much information the human brain can retain and understand at a given time. This is particularly true when a person tries to remember all of the variables in a rapidly changing environment. This concept is referred to as bounded rationality. According to Oliver Williamson:

"Bounded rationality involves neuro-physiological limits on the one hand and language limits on the other. The physical limits take the form of rate and storage limits on the powers of individuals to receive, store, and process information without error. Language limits refer to the inability of individuals to articulate their knowledge or feelings by use of words, numbers, or graphics in ways which permit them to be understood by others. Despite their best efforts, parties may find that language fails them (possibly because they do not possess the requisite vocabulary or the necessary vocabulary has not been devised) and they resort to other means of communication instead." (Afuah 39)

The second principle is that any program structure can be expressed as a combination of basic building blocks. These blocks include Sequence Statements (a set of instructions executed in the order that they are written), Selection Statements (IF, THEN, ELSE constructs that allows a choice of processing paths) and Iteration Statements (DO WHILE, DO UNTIL, LOOP, SEARCH).

The third principle is the concept that modules should have a single-entry point and a single exit point. This type of structure eliminates the need for the GO TO instruction..

The fourth principle is that a hierarchical concept should be used for the design of program logic under control of sequence, selection, and iteration statements. This hierarchical design can be achieved by parsing the larger program into smaller modules, starting at the top of the problem, and working our way down.

While these articles began the "structured revolution" they did not provide a formal definition of structured programming. But from this study, the author has developed the following definition. Structured programming is the stepwise process of parsing program functions into a hierarchical chain of modules. Each of these modules perform a single task, are efficient and economical, contain the basic constructs of sequence, selection, and repetition, are free of GOTO processing, have a single entrance point, have a single exit point, have a minimum number of control statements, eliminate programming tricks, and are used to produce provable, reliable software systems.

There are several phases of structured programming. In each of these phases we take a higher level concept and parse it into subordinate, elemental portions. The first phase is structured analysis. This is where we research and define what the user really wants, as opposed to what he asked for (which are often two entirely different things). The results of structured analysis should be the requirements definition, which contains lists of what the resulting systems and programs will do. The requirements definitions can be expressed with narratives, decision tables, and logical dataflow diagrams.

The structured design phase is used to split the requirements into their individual modules. We then split the resulting modules into their individual functions. The resulting design documents will include physical dataflow diagrams, program specifications, screen and report examples, testing requirements, and prototyping.

In the structured coding phase we translate the program specifications into fully functional programs. Structured coding includes two areas, readability coding and modular coding.

In the readability coding phase we ensure that the next person who has to read this program will be able to understand it. This includes indented coding, delimiter coding and blank line insertions, one line per condition, data name conventions, module labeling, and adherence to shop standards.

In the modular coding we ensure that the program functions are grouped into the proper modules, using a minimal number of program control structures. This modularization is the kernel of structured programming. The whole point of structured programming is to improve program correctness. The easiest way to do this is to minimize the number of things that can wrong. Remember "Murphy was an optimist!".

In the structured testing is where we test each individual modules, and then test the interfaces between the modules. All of this testing is done according to the test plan that we developed during the design phase.

Structured documentation is built from both the System specifications and the testing results.

We can also see that the entire concept of Structured Programming is a hierarchical process. This structure can be seen in the following adaptation of a waterfall diagram:

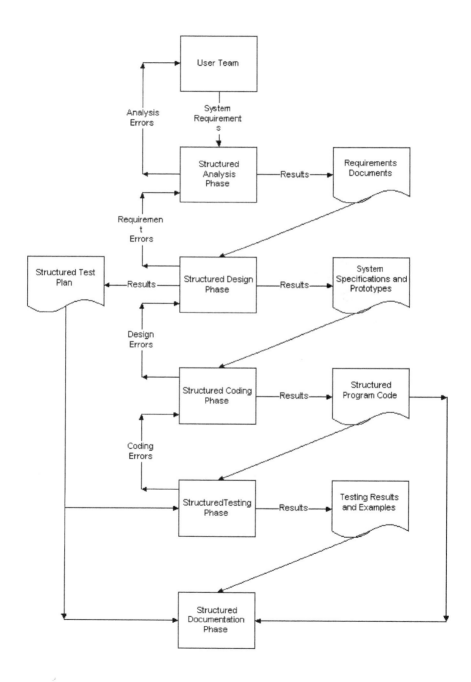

As we can see from this diagram, we take in the high level user needs and through a parsing process we can produce the functioning system. If any of these steps is skipped the project will not be successful. If we skip or shorten the analysis step then we will miss some of the user's requirements, and the system we will not meet their needs. If we skip or shorten the design step we will produce a system that is unfriendly and difficult to use and understand. If we skip or shorten the coding step, we will lose functionally, and will have to spend maintenance time restoring functions and correcting data errors. If we skip or shorten the testing step the system will be unreliable. If we skip or shorten the documentation step the system will become inflexible because after awhile no one will know what it does, much less how to change it.

But by using structured programming to break complex ideas into simpler parts, it is easier to apply changes to individual parts and to understand the total situation. This allows us to:

1) improve the effectiveness of our programs, because the user will understand the programs function before it is built, and determine if it will fulfill his needs.

2) improve the accuracy of our programs by proving that all parts of the program are correct before the user sees the program in the production environment.

3) improve our ability to meet delivery schedules by simplifying the development process.

4) lengthen the active life of the program by making it easier to change and maintain.

5) improve the performance of the program by simplifying its function through the elimination of redundant code, and the minimization of logic control processing.

6) improve morale of the programming team by allowing them to work on programs that are easy to maintain and change.

7) improve morale of the development team by allowing them to produce high quality programs and systems.

8) decrease programming cost by developing modules that can be used by multiple applications.

In the rest of this book we will concentrate on the structured coding phase of structured programming.

References

Afuah, Allken and Tucci, Christopher L. <u>Internet Business Models and Strategies</u> 2001
McGraw Hill New York

Chapter 2

Parsing of Functions

In our definition of structured programming, we said that it is "a stepwise process of parsing program functions into a hierarchical chain of modules". In this chapter we will discuss this parsing process. In parsing, we take a complicated item and break it into its component pieces. We can call each of these component pieces a unit of work.

In physics, work is defined as the force required to move an object across a specific distance. We can use this concept to define a unit of work as the collection of the input of force against the object, the process of moving the object, the rules that effect the objects motion, and the results of the object's movement. Think about shooting a basketball. We can examine this action using our definition of a unit of work.

The input of force against the object.
• The energy of your throw.

The process of moving the object.
• How well you aim your throw.
• How well you execute your throw.

The rules that effect the objects motion.
• The results of bouncing the ball off the backboard.

- The actions of the defense trying to block the shot.
- The effects of friction and gravity on the ball's trajectory.
- The effects of the ball's spin on its accuracy.

The results of the object's movement.
- The three point game winning shot from half court as the closing buzzer sounds.

Applying this definition to the programming world, we can say that a unit of work is the collection of the input of data into a process, the process of moving the data to the output, the algorithm rules that must be obeyed, and the resulting output from the process.

Units of work can be seen at many different levels of processing. For example, we can review the following processes; a system that manages a company's order entry and order processing, the maintenance screen of the order entry system that adds a new customer; and the process of editing the state code of the billing address.

Here we will examine the system that manages a company's order entry and order processing:

The input of data into a process.
- List of customers.
- List of items, and their prices.
- The available quantities of these items, and their location.

The process of moving the data to the output.
- Creation of a list of valid customers.
- Creation of a list of valid items, their price, their availability, and their location.
- Taking of the customer order.
- Collection and disbursement of the material.
- Reordering of depleted inventory.

- Preparation and mailing of customer invoices.
- Processing of accounts receivable for customer invoices.

The algorithm rules that must be obeyed.
- Customer must be on the database before they can place an order.
- Items must be on the database before they can be ordered.
- Items must be in stock before they can be shipped.
- The customer must have a good payment record before orders can be accepted.

The resulting output from the process.
- Warehouse pick lists
- Shipped orders.
- Out of stock lists.
- Purchasing orders.
- Customer invoices and statements.
- Payment for inventories received.
- A history of customer orders.

Here we can examine the maintenance screen of the order entry system that adds a new customer :

The input of data into a process.
- The customer number.
- The customer name.
- The customer's billing address.
- The customer's ship to address.

The process of moving the data to the output
- a new database record is created
- the screen fields are copied to the positions on the database record.

<u>The algorithm rules that must be obeyed.</u>
- The customer must not already exist.
- Certain fields (ie. customer's name) must be filled in.
- Only certain codes are valid in the state field.

<u>The resulting output from the process.</u>
- The new database record.

Here we can examine the process of editing the state code of the billing address.

<u>The input of data into a process.</u>
- The state code from the screen.

<u>The process of moving the data to the output.</u>
- Check the state code against the list of valid state codes.
- Set a flag if a valid code is not found.
- Prepare an error message.

<u>The algorithm rules that must be obeyed.</u>
- The state code filed must be populated.
- Only certain codes are valid.

<u>The resulting output from the process.</u>
- An error message is sent to the user.
- The literal containing the full state name, which can be displayed on the screen.

Each unit of work is part of a higher level. In parsing we examine each level, and reduce it to a set of simpler units of work. This is what we have done in our examples above. The ultimate goal is to produce what we can call an elemental units of work.

An elemental unit of work has the following characteristics. First it has a single input source. This could be a row of a table or the fields from an input record. Second, it has a single process, such as loading the fields of an output record, populating a report line, or adding a row to a table. Third, the rules of an elemental unit of work that govern that process all relate directly to the output that is being generated. These rules include the IF statements that choose a value, or some minor computations. The fourth characteristic is that there is a single output, such as a single report line or a single output record.

It is at the elemental level that programming really works. In fact, we can say that the art of structured coding consists of: the refining of stated needs into elemental units of work and then combining of the elemental units of work into a structured hierarchy.

We can see how this is done be writing an algorithm about how to build a peanut butter sandwich. We begin by determining what the major processes are in building a sandwich and defining them as units of work:

Process 1—Get the bread.

Input	• Bread in a bag in the bread box
Process	• Open the bread box.
	• Check for bread.
	• Open the bag.
	• Check the condition of the bread. It cannot be moldy, stale, or wet.
	• Remove the bread.
	• Close the bag.
	• Return the bag.
	• Close the bread box.
Rules	• The bread box must be present.
	• We must be able to open the bread box.
	• The bread must be in the bag.
	• The bread cannot be moldy, or wet, or stale.
Output	• Two slices of bread.

Process 2—Get the peanut butter.

Input	• Peanut butter from the pantry.
Process	• Open the pantry.
	• Check for peanut butter.
	• Open the peanut butter jar.
	• Check that the jar is not empty.
Rules	• The peanut butter must be present.
	• The jar must be easy to open.
Output	• Opened peanut butter jar.

Process 3—Get the jelly.

Input	• Jelly from the refrigerator.
Process	• Open the refrigerator.
	• Check for jelly.
	• Open the jelly jar.
	• Check that the jar is not empty.
Rules	• The jelly must be present.
	• The jar must be easy to open.
Output	• Opened jelly jar.

Process 4—Get a knife from the drawer.

Input	• Knife from the drawer.
Process	• Open the drawer.
	• Check for a knife.
	• Remove the knife.
	• Check that the knife is clean.
Rules	• The knife must be present.
	• The knife must be clean.
Output	• A clean knife.

Process 5—Apply the peanut butter to the bread.
Input
- Peanut butter.
- Bread.
- Knife.

Process
- Lay the bread on the counter.
- Use the knife to remove the peanut butter.
- Use the knife to apply the peanut butter to the bread.

Rules
- Only apply the peanut butter to one side of the bread.

Output
- Bread with one side covered with peanut butter.

Process 6—Apply the jelly to the bread
Input
- Jelly
- Bread
- Knife

Process
- Lay the bread on the counter
- Use the knife to remove the jelly
- Use the knife to apply the jelly to the bread

Rules
- Only apply the jelly to one side of the bread
- Don't use the same piece of bread that the peanut butter is on.

Output
- Bread with one side covered with jelly.

Process 7—Put the two pieces together.
Input
- One piece of bread with jelly on it.
- One piece of bread with peanut butter on it.

Process
- Leave one piece of bread with peanut butter on the counter.
- Pick up the piece of bread with the jelly on it.
- Turn the bread in your hand over so that the jelly side is down.
- Place the two pieces of bread together.

Rules
- The sticky sides go together.
- The two parts need to be lined up correctly.

Output
- One peanut butter and jelly sandwich.

Now that we have defined the seven individual units of work, we need to figure out how to combine them back into a single process. We will do this by taking these individual units of work, and give them computer like names:

GET-THE BREAD
GET-THE-PEANUT-BUTTER
GET-THE-JELLY
GET-A-KNIFE
APPLY-THE-PEANUT-BUTTER
APPLY-THE-JELLY
PUT-THE-TWO-PIECES-TOGETHER

This list can give us an outline of the "program". By reading this list we not only see what will happen, and the order that it will happen in. The order of course is important because certain actions (APPLY-THE-JELLY) are dependant on the completion of certain other actions (GET-THE-BREAD, GET-THE-JELLY, GET-A-KNIFE). We can examine all of these dependencies by drawing the following simple diagram:

Figure 2.1—Dependency Diagram

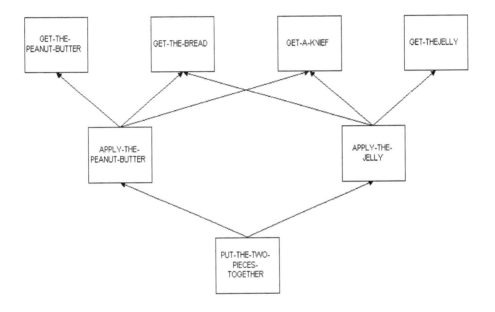

Figure 2.1

We learn two things about the process from this diagram. The first point is that the units of work on each level are dependent on the completion of some or all of the units of work on the proceeding level. This is because one task (APPLY-THE-JELLY) cannot be started until an earlier task (GET-THE-JELLY) is completed. (The only exception is the author's seven year old daughter Tami, who doesn't like jelly on her sandwich.

The second point is that the units of work on each level are independent of each other. We can complete APPLY-THE-JELLY without completing APPLY-THE-PEANUT-BUTTER. The status of GET-A-KNIFE does not effect GET-THE-BREAD. This allows us to reorder the boxes to make the diagram easier to read (and to draw). From this, we can expand our "program" to include these dependencies.

```
DO GET-THE BREAD
DO GET-THE-PEANUT-BUTTER
DO GET-THE-JELLY
DO GET-A-KNIFE

IF    GET-THE BREAD              WAS SUCCESSFUL
AND GET-THE-PEANUT-BUTTER   WAS SUCCESSFUL
AND GET-A-KNIFE                 WAS SUCCESSFUL
     DO APPLY-THE-PEANUT-BUTTER
END-IF

IF    GET-THE BREAD              WAS SUCCESSFUL
AND GET-THE-JELLY               WAS SUCCESSFUL
AND GET-A-KNIFE                 WAS SUCCESSFUL
     DO APPLY-THE-JELLY
END-IF

IF    GET-THE BREAD              WAS SUCCESSFUL
AND GET-THE-PEANUT-BUTTER   WAS SUCCESSFUL
AND GET-THE-JELLY               WAS SUCCESSFUL
AND GET-A-KNIFE                 WAS SUCCESSFUL
AND APPLY-THE-PEANUT-BUTTER  WAS SUCCESSFUL
AND APPLY-THE-JELLY             WAS SUCCESSFUL
     DO PUT-THE-TWO-PIECES-TOGETHER
END-IF
```

Note that because the APPLY-THE-JELLY function does not depend on GET-THE-PEANUT-BUTTER function, it is in a separate paragraph from APPLY-THE-PEANUT-BUTTER function.

As we pointed out in the first chapter, one of the characteristics of a good program is efficiency. In our program it would be a waste of resources to do GET-THE-JELLY if we cannot complete GET-THE-BREAD. This quest for efficiency expands our program as follows:

```
DO GET-THE BREAD

IF    GET-THE BREAD              WAS SUCCESSFUL
      DO GET-THE-PEANUT-BUTTER
END-IF

IF    GET-THE BREAD              WAS SUCCESSFUL
AND GET-THE-PEANUT-BUTTER   WAS SUCCESSFUL
      DO GET-THE-JELLY
END-IF

IF    GET-THE BREAD              WAS SUCCESSFUL
AND GET-THE-PEANUT-BUTTER   WAS SUCCESSFUL
AND GET-THE-JELLY             WAS SUCCESSFUL
      DO GET-A-KNIFE
END-IF

IF    GET-THE BREAD              WAS SUCCESSFUL
AND GET-THE-PEANUT-BUTTER   WAS SUCCESSFUL
AND GET-A-KNIFE              WAS SUCCESSFUL
      DO APPLY-THE-PEANUT-BUTTER
END-IF

IF    GET-THE BREAD              WAS SUCCESSFUL
AND GET-THE-JELLY             WAS SUCCESSFUL
AND GET-A-KNIFE              WAS SUCCESSFUL
      DO APPLY-THE-JELLY
END-IF
```

```
IF    GET-THE BREAD               WAS SUCCESSFUL
AND GET-THE-PEANUT-BUTTER  WAS SUCCESSFUL
AND GET-THE-JELLY               WAS SUCCESSFUL
AND GET-A-KNIFE                  WAS SUCCESSFUL
AND APPLY-THE-PEANUT-BUTTER WAS SUCCESSFUL
AND APPLY-THE-JELLY             WAS SUCCESSFUL
     DO PUT-THE-TWO-PIECES-TOGETHER
END-IF
```

But remember that Tami doesn't like want jelly on her sandwich. (There's always something.) This means that if we are making a sandwich for Tami, we must skip the two jelly steps. So we have to add this exception to our "program".

```
DO GET-THE BREAD

IF    GET-THE BREAD               WAS SUCCESSFUL
     DO GET-THE-PEANUT-BUTTER
END-IF

IF THIS-IS-TAMI'S-SANDWICH
   SKIP THIS STEP
ELSE
   IF    GET-THE BREAD               WAS SUCCESSFUL
   AND GET-THE-PEANUT-BUTTER  WAS SUCCESSFUL
        DO GET-THE-JELLY
   END-IF
END-IF

IF    GET-THE BREAD               WAS SUCCESSFUL
AND GET-THE-PEANUT-BUTTER  WAS SUCCESSFUL
     IF    GET-THE-JELLY           WAS SUCCESSFUL
     OR  THIS-IS-TAMI'S-SANDWICH
          DO GET-A-KNIFE
     END-IF
END-IF
```

```
IF    GET-THE BREAD                WAS SUCCESSFUL
AND GET-THE-PEANUT-BUTTER    WAS SUCCESSFUL
AND GET-A-KNIFE                WAS SUCCESSFUL
    DO APPLY-THE-PEANUT-BUTTER
END-IF

IF THIS-IS-TAMI'S-SANDWICH
    SKIP THIS STEP
ELSE
    IF    GET-THE BREAD            WAS SUCCESSFUL
    AND GET-THE-JELLY             WAS SUCCESSFUL
    AND GET-A-KNIFE               WAS SUCCESSFUL
        DO APPLY-THE-JELLY
    END-IF
END-IF

IF    GET-THE BREAD               WAS SUCCESSFUL
AND GET-THE-PEANUT-BUTTER    WAS SUCCESSFUL
AND GET-A-KNIFE               WAS SUCCESSFUL
AND APPLY-THE-PEANUT-BUTTER  WAS SUCCESSFUL
    IF  THIS-IS-TAMI'S-SANDWICH
        DO PUT-THE-TWO-PIECES-TOGETHER
    ELSE
        IF  GET-THE-JELLY         WAS SUCCESSFUL
        AND APPLY-THE-JELLY       WAS SUCCESSFUL
            DO PUT-THE-TWO-PIECES-TOGETHER
        END-IF
    END-IF
END-IF
```

Now this gives us a lot of flags to contend with. But we really only have two conditions to deal with; "is this Tami's sandwich", and "should we continue the process, or has a problem been encountered". Because all of the "WAS SUCCESSFUL" flags are all used to determine if the process should continue, we can replace them with a single question. Each sub process will change this flag to "NO" if a problem is encountered. This change allows us to simplify our program as follows:

```
MOVE "YES" TO CONTINUE-PROCESS
DO GET-THE BREAD

IF CONTINUE-PROCESS    = "YES"
   DO GET-THE-PEANUT-BUTTER
END-IF

IF CONTINUE-PROCESS = "YES"
   IF THIS-IS-TAMI'S-SANDWICH
      SKIP THIS STEP
   ELSE
      DO GET-THE-JELLY
   END-IF
END-IF

IF CONTINUE-PROCESS    = "YES"
   DO GET-A-KNIFE
END-IF

IF CONTINUE-PROCESS    = "YES"
   DO APPLY-THE-PEANUT-BUTTER
END-IF

IF CONTINUE-PROCESS = "YES"
   IF THIS-IS-TAMI'S-SANDWICH
      SKIP THIS STEP
   ELSE
      DO APPLY-THE-JELLY
   END-IF
END-IF

IF CONTINUE-PROCESS    = "YES"
   DO PUT-THE-TWO-PIECES-TOGETHER
END-IF
```

With this "program" we have translated the human's defined task "build a peanut butter sandwich" into an algorithm that a computer could understand. We did this in two steps. First we parsed the task into individual units of work, striving to produce elemental units of work. Then we combined these units of work into a hierarchy that recognizes the dependencies between the units of work.

When we compare this "program" to the list of characteristics of a good program that we defined in chapter 1 we find that it qualifies. First, the program is effective. When executed, it will produce a peanut butter sandwich. Second, the program is available on time, as it is was finished in time to be included in this text. Third, the program can be easily changed. If Tami starts wanting jelly on her sandwich, then we can simply remove those exception references. This change will not effect any other part of the program. Fourth, the program is efficient, in that unnecessary steps will be skipped if a previous steps fails.

In the next chapter we will discuss a more formal method of deriving units of work, and the hierarchy that connects them. But with all of this talk of sandwiches, it's now time for the lunch.

Chapter 3

Coupling and Cohesion

Everyone agrees that structured programming is important. But not everyone agrees on what constitutes a structured program. I have had discussions with people who defend the structure of a program which contains 40 GO TO commands. I have seen "structured programs" with paragraphs that run on for ten pages. Many of these arguments were emotional, based more on style than any formal dynamic.

But there is a way to evaluate the "structure" of a program by measuring the program's use of coupling and cohesion. Coupling is the measure of the strength of the connection between modules of program code. The level of coupling between two modules can be measured by the amount of understanding the programmer must have about one module to be able to understand the function of the other module. There are three levels of coupling.

1) DATA COUPLING is the most desirable form of coupling. Data is passed to a module to begin the processing of that module or to return control to the calling module.

2) CONTROL COUPLING is the second level of coupling, and is not as acceptable as data coupling. In this type of coupling a flag is passed up or down the program hierarchy to control the processing of the receiving module.

3) PATHOLOGICAL COUPLING, as its name infers, is the worst type of coupling. The first module may extract some data from the second, change it, or branch to some specific instruction in the second module or to an different module, based on some control value.

To obtain the best level of coupling we want to minimize the amount of control that is passed between modules. First we want to minimize the amount of control that the calling module has on the called module. One way is to minimize the number and complexity of the control flags that are passed from one module to the next. We don't want a situation where we send two control flags to a routine, one of which modifies the other, when we can send one control flag. For example, if we have a date conversion routine, we need to tell it what to do (convert date, edit date, etc.), the type of date we are passing (Gregorian, Julian, Military), and in a conversion request the type of date we want back. We can accomplish this with either three flags or one flag.

Version 1—Passing three control parms.

```
01  DATE-ROUTINE-CONTROL.
    05  PROCESS-TYPE           PIC X(01).
        88  CONVERT-DATE                VALUE 'C'.
        88  EDIT-DATE                   VALUE 'E'.
    05  INPUT-DATE-TYPE        PIC X(01).
        88  GREGORIAN-DATE              VALUE 'G'.
        88  JULIAN-DATE                 VALUE 'J'.
        88  MILITARY-DATE               VALUE 'M'.
    05  OUTPUT-DATE-TYPE       PIC X(01).
        88  GREGORIAN-DATE              VALUE 'G'.
        88  JULIAN-DATE                 VALUE 'J'.
        88  MILITARY-DATE               VALUE 'M'.
```

Version 2—Passing one control parm.

```
01  DATE-ROUTINE-CONTROL.
    05  PROCESS-TYPE          PIC X(02).
        88  CONVERT-GREGORIAN-JULIAN        VALUE '01'.
        88  CONVERT-GREGORIAN-MILITARY      VALUE '02'.
        88  CONVERT-JULIAN-GREGORIAN        VALUE '03'.
        88  CONVERT-JULIAN-MILITARY         VALUE '04'.
        88  CONVERT-MILITARY-JULIAN         VALUE '05'.
        88  CONVERT-MILITARY-GREGORIAN      VALUE '06'.
        88  EDIT-DATE-GREGORIAN             VALUE '07'.
        88  EDIT-DATE-JULIAN                VALUE '08'.
        88  EDIT-DATE-MILITARY              VALUE '09'.
```

By using version 2, we simplify the control logic of the called program by giving it a single value to evaluate. Using version 1, the called program would have to determine if the combination of three flags is valid, and then determine what to do. Using version 2 also allows the calling program to have a single point where it sets the control flags, rather than setting three control flags.

We also want to minimize the amount of control data that is returned from the called module. For example, we can have a subroutine that reads a database table and returns the results. We could either use two flags or one flag to tell the calling program the status of the request.

Version 1—Using two results flags.

```
01  DB-RETURN-CONTROL.
    05  DBCALL-RETURN-FLAG       PIC X(02).
        88  GOOD-RETURN-CALL            VALUE '00'.
        88  PROCESS-ERROR-FOUND         VALUE '01'.
    05  RECORD-FOUND-FLAG        PIC X(01).
        88  RECORD-FOUND                VALUE 'Y'.
        88  RECORD-NOT-FOUND            VALUE 'N'.
```

Version 2—Using one results flag.

```
01  DB-RETURN-CONTROL.
    05  DBCALL-RETURN-FLAG          PIC X(02).
        88  RECORD-FOUND                    VALUE '00'.
        88  RECORD-NOT-FOUND                VALUE '01'.
        88  PROCESS-ERROR-FOUND             VALUE '02'.
```

Again version 2 is better because the calling program only needs to evaluate one flag rather than two flags. This will also simplify the called program which will only have to set one return code flag.

The opposite of coupling is cohesion. Whereas coupling is a measure of independence of modules, cohesion is the measure of the glue that binds the functions within modules together. There are seven levels of cohesion.

1) FUNCTIONAL COHESION is the best in that all of the functions in the module contribute directly to the accomplishment of a single task.

2) SEQUENTIAL COHESION serves as a gateway to the other modules in the system. Typically, a sequentially cohesive module starts one module, regains control from it when it is done, and passes some data on to a third module. This type of module often serves as a control point for the program.

3) COMMUNICATIONAL COHESION happens when separate functions that work on common data are grouped in the same module.

4) PROCEDURAL COHESION is present when modules are grouped together because they follow the flow of control in a program. This type of cohesion often occurs when programs are coded from traditional flow charts.

5) TEMPORAL COHESION happens when functions are grouped together merely because they happen at the same time.

6) LOGICAL COHESION happens when functions are grouped together simply because they do similar functions to the same data. The choice of the logic path to be followed is based on a control character that is set somewhere else in the program.

7) COINCIDENTAL COHESION occurs when functions just happen to be together because of some arbitrary decision.

With these definitions in mind, we can review and discuss code fragments that show examples of these different types of cohesion. The following paragraph is an example of functional cohesion.

```
X100-READ-INPUT-FILE.
    READ 100-INPUT-FILE INTO 900-INPUT-RECORD
        AT END MOVE 'Y' TO 310-END-OF-FILE-FLAG.
    IF 310-END-OF-FILE-FLAG NOT EQUAL 'Y'
        ADD 1 TO 300-INPUT-RECORDS-READ.
```

When a module has functional cohesion, all of the parts of the module contribute to a single function. In the example above, we are reading an input file into the working storage area that defines the record layout. This function consists of reading the input file, loading the working storage area, checking for end of file, setting the end of file flag, and incrementing the input counter. But each of these elementary tasks contribute to the larger function of reading the input record. Modules that are functionally cohesive are able to complete a elemental unit of work as we defined it in Chanter 2.

The following paragraph is an example of sequential cohesion.

```
A100-BUILD-GRADE-TABLE.
    MOVE 'N' TO 310-END-OF-GRADE-FILE-FG.
    OPEN INPUT 100-GRADE-FILE.
    PERFORM X300-READ-GRADE-FILE.
    PERFORM A110-BUILD-GRADE-TABLE
        UNTIL 310-END-OF-GRADE-FILE-FG = 'Y'.
    CLOSE 100-GRADE-FILE.
```

This module is a control point in the program. It's purpose is to control the loading of a file into an internal program table for later processing. This process consists of initializing the END-OF-FILE control flag, opening the input file, calling the module that reads the first record in the file, calling the module that processes the loading of the table, and closing the input file. The module controls the processing of the input file, but does not actually read the file, or load the table.

A sequentially cohesive paragraph can be use to control the execution of a series of functionally cohesive modules. The paragraph then serves as an outline of the program. A programmer can then query the individual functionally cohesive modules for more detail about specific program functions. Using the combination of these two types of modules will give us the best results.

The following paragraph is an example of communicational cohesion. Here, we are using different functions to load an output file record:

```
B310-LOAD-OUTPUT-RECORD.
    MOVE GTR-C-STR-NBR              TO GSG-C-STR-NBR.
    MOVE GTR-C-TNK-NBR              TO GSG-C-TNK-NBR.
    MOVE 350-CURRENT-CCYYMMDD TO GSG-C-EFFECTIVE-DATE.
    ADD  1                         TO GSG-RECORD-NUMBER.
    COMPUTE GSG-GRADE-RATIO
           = GTR-TOTAL-FUEL / GTR-BASE-FUEL.
    MOVE 'OTH'                     TO GSG-GRADE-TYPE
    MOVE 'O'                       TO GSG-BASE-GRADE.
    MOVE 350-CURRENT-HHMMSS   TO GSG-TIME-STAMP.
```

We load the entire output record using values from another record, values from WORKING-STORAGE fields, the results of an ADD statement, the results of a COMPUTE statement, and alphanumeric littorals. But all of the target fields are defined in the same output record layout. This means that the module is solving a single variable.

The following paragraph is an example of procedural cohesion. Here we group functions because they follow the procedural flow of the program.

```
0010-READ-JRNLMEIN.
     READ JRNLMEIN
        AT END CLOSE JRNLMEIN
             GO TO 0100-READ-GAS002D.

0015-WRITE-JRNLMEDT.
     IF CLOSE-FLAG = 'ON'
        MOVE JRNL-MEIN TO JRNL-MEOT
        WRITE JRNL-MEOT
         GO TO 0010-READ-JRNLMEIN.
     MOVE JRNL-MEIN TO JRN-TRANS-REC.
     WRITE JRN-TRANS-REC.
     GO TO 0010-READ-JRNLMEIN.

0100-READ-GAS002D.
     READ GAS002D
        AT END MOVE 'ON' TO GAS002D-EOF
             GO TO 0105-EXIT.
     IF GAS-TRANS = 2
        NEXT SENTENCE
     ELSE
        GO TO 0100-READ-GAS002D.
0105-EXIT.
     EXIT.

0110-CHECK-EOF.
     IF GAS002D-EOF = 'ON'
        NEXT SENTENCE
     ELSE
        GO TO 0120-CONVERT-PO.
```

```
        CLOSE GAS002D.
        DISPLAY ' JOURNALS OUT: '.
        GOBACK.

0120-CONVERT-PO.
        MOVE GAS-PO-NUM TO WS-PO-NUM.
        IF WS-7 NUMERIC
            MOVE WS-7 TO PO-NUM
            GO TO 0130-CONVERT-GRADE.
        IF WS-6 NUMERIC
            MOVE WS-6 TO PO-NUM
            GO TO 0130-CONVERT-GRADE.
        IF WS-5 NUMERIC
            MOVE WS-5 TO PO-NUM
            GO TO 0130-CONVERT-GRADE.
        IF WS-4 NUMERIC
            MOVE WS-4 TO PO-NUM
            GO TO 0130-CONVERT-GRADE.
        IF WS-3 NUMERIC
            MOVE WS-3 TO PO-NUM
            GO TO 0130-CONVERT-GRADE.
        IF WS-2 NUMERIC
            MOVE WS-2 TO PO-NUM
            GO TO 0130-CONVERT-GRADE.
        DISPLAY ' INVALID PO-NUMBER '
        GO TO 0100-READ-GAS002D.

    0130-CONVERT-GRADE.
        .
        .
        .
        GO TO 0100-READ-GAS002D.
```

Procedural cohesion usually results when the code is written from a flow chart. We can see this correlation by examining a flow chart that was built from this code.

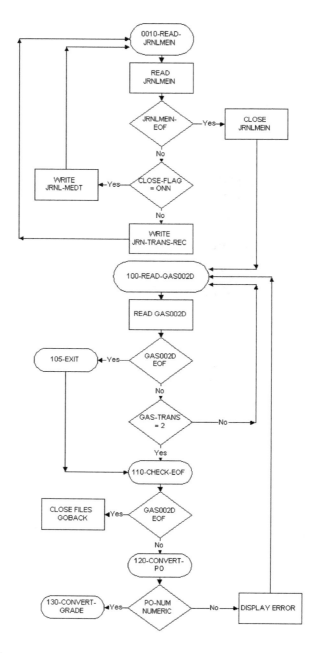

Figure 3.1

As we said earlier, procedural cohesion is less acceptable than functional, sequential, and communicational cohesion. By reworking this example into higher level of cohesion, we can produce the following code:

```
B100-PROCESS-PROCEDURAL.
    PERFORM X100-READ-JRNLMEIN.
    PERFORM B110-PROCESS-JRNLMEIN
        UNTIL EOF-JRNLMEIN = 'Y'.
    CLOSE JRNLMEIN.

    PERFORM X200-READ-GAS002D.
    PERFORM B120-PROCESS-GAS002D
        UNTIL EOF-GAS002D  = 'Y'
            OR GAS-TRAN    = 2.

    CLOSE GAS002D.
    DISPLAY ' JOURNALS OUT: '.
    GOBACK.

B110-PROCESS-JRNLMEIN.
    MOVE JRNL-MEIN TO JRN-TRANS-REC.
    WRITE JRN-TRANS-REC.
    PERFORM X100-READ-JRNLMEIN.

B120-PROCESS-GAS002D.
    PERFORM B121-EDIT-PO-NUM.
    IF PO-NUM GREATER THAN SPACES
        PERFORM B123-CONVERT-GRADE.
    PERFORM X200-READ-GAS002D.

B121-EDIT-PO-NUM.
    MOVE SPACES TO PO-NUM
    IF WS-2 NUMERIC
        MOVE WS-2 TO PO-NUM.
    IF WS-3 NUMERIC
        MOVE WS-3 TO PO-NUM.
    IF WS-4 NUMERIC
        MOVE WS-4 TO PO-NUM.
```

```
        IF WS-5 NUMERIC
            MOVE WS-5 TO PO-NUM.
        IF WS-6 NUMERIC
            MOVE WS-6 TO PO-NUM.
        IF WS-7 NUMERIC
            MOVE WS-7 TO PO-NUM.
        IF PO-NUM = SPACES
            DISPLAY ' INVALID PO-NUMBER '.


    B123-CONVERT-GRADE.


    X100-READ-JRNLMEIN.
        READ JRNLMEIN
            AT END MOVE 'Y' TO EOF-JRNLMEIN.


    X200-READ-GAS002D.
        READ GAS002D
            AT END MOVE 'Y' TO EOF-GAS002D.
```

Reviewing the changes, we see that we first created functionally cohesive modules for the two read processes (X100-READ-JRNLMEIN, X200-READ-GAS002D). Then we moved the editing of the PO-NUM to a new functionally cohesive module (B121-EDIT-PO-NUM). Then we built the sequentially cohesive modules B100-PROCESS-FUNC-TIONAL, B110-PROCESS-JRNLMEIN, B120-PROCESS-GAS002D. And finally we reversed the loading of the PO-NUM field, and used the field as its own processing flag.

We can see a number of improvements in the program as a result of these changes. First we have shortened the program by 9 lines. Second, we discover that the processing of the JRNLMEIN and the GAS002D files are independent. When we first looked at this program, we assumed that they were interrelated. And third we discover that the IF statement check in the original paragraph 0015-WRITE-JRNLMEDT is never true, since CLOSE- FLAG is related to the processing if the GAS002D file. We can then delete this code, making the program easier to understand. Again example we can see that we can improve the readability of the program by using higher levels of cohesion.

The following paragraph is an example of temporal cohesion.

```
8000-READ-GM1-FILE.
    READ GM1-FILE-IN INTO GM1-RECORD
        AT END MOVE 'T' TO WS-END-OF-FILE-FLAG
            GO TO 8000-EXIT.

    ADD 1 TO WS-GM1-RECS-READ
    IF WS-GM1-RECS-READ < 25
        DISPLAY 'INP —' GM1-RECORD.
    IF GM1-G-KEY = WS-GM1-KEY(1)
        IF WS-GM1-RECS-DROP < 25
            DISPLAY ' DROP—' GM1-RECORD.

    IF GM1-G-KEY = WS-GM1-KEY(1)
        MOVE GM1-RECORD TO WS-GM1-REC(1)
        ADD 1 TO WS-GM1-RECS-DROP.

    IF GM1-G-KEY NOT = WS-GM1-KEY(1)
        PERFORM 7000-WRITE-GM1 THRU 7000-EXIT
        MOVE GM1-RECORD TO WS-GM1-REC(1).

8000-EXIT.
    EXIT.
```

The programmer who wrote this code decided that since these functions; reading the input file, displaying the first 25 input records, displaying the first 25 dropped records, incrementing the drop count on duplicate records, and performing paragraph 7000-WRITE-GM1 to write out the unique records, all occur at the same time, that they should be grouped together. However, since we have redundant IF statements, there might be a better way to group these statements. Restructuring these paragraphs gives the following results:

```
B100-PROCESS-TEMPORAL.
    PERFORM X100-READ-GM1-RECORD.
    PERFORM B110-PROCESS-TEMPORAL.
        UNTIL WS-END-OF-FILE-FLAG = 'T'.

B110-PROCESS-TEMPORAL.
    IF WS-GM1-RECS-READ < 25
        DISPLAY 'INP —' GM1-RECORD.
    IF GM1-G-KEY = WS-GM1-KEY(1)
        PERFORM B111-PROCESS-DUPLICATE
    ELSE
        PERFORM 7000-WRITE-GM1 THRU 7000-EXIT.
    MOVE GM1-RECORD TO WS-GM1-REC(1).
    PERFORM X100-READ-GM1-RECORD.

B111-PROCESS-DUPLICATES.
    IF WS-GM1-RECS-DROP < 25
        DISPLAY ' DROP—' GM1-RECORD.
    ADD 1 TO WS-GM1-RECS-DROP.

X100-READ-GM1-RECORD.
    READ GM1-FILE-IN INTO GM1-RECORD
        AT END MOVE 'T' TO WS-END-OF-FILE-FLAG.
    IF WS-END-OF-FILE-FLAG NOT EQUAL 'T'
        ADD 1 TO WS-GM1-RECS-READ.
```

Reviewing the changes, we see that we began by building a functional cohesive module to process the duplicate records (B100-PROCESS-DUPLICATES). We then built a functional cohesive module to handle the actual read processing (X100-READ-GM1-RECORD). And finally we built a sequential cohesive module to control the processing of the other modules. These changes allowed us to eliminate the duplicate checks of the GM1-G-KEY against the WS-GM1-KEY(1).

We are also able to eliminate the GO TO processing by isolating the record processing from the read driver. In our new code, we initialize the loop by performing the first read. We then changed B110-PROCESS-

TEMPORAL to include the process to perform the main processing, get the next record, and check for end of file (with the UNTIL clause of the PERFORM statement). If the end of file flag was tripped, we will end the processing. Since we check for end of file before we process the data, there is no need for the GO TO statement.

The following paragraph is an example of logical cohesion.

```
IF 310-VALID-AGAINST-GVC = 'Y'
    MOVE GSG-D-EFF-DTE        TO 605-GSG-D-EFF-DTE
    MOVE GSG-C-GRD-BASE       TO 605-GSG-C-GRD-BASE
    MOVE GSG-C-GRD-TYPE       TO 605-GSG-C-GRD-TYPE
ELSE
    MOVE ZEROES               TO 605-GSG-D-EFF-DTE
    MOVE SPACES               TO 605-GSG-C-GRD-BASE
    MOVE SPACES               TO 605-GSG-C-GRD-TYPE.
```

This code fragment is an example of logical cohesion because the flag 310-VALID-AGAINST-GVC, which was set in another part of the program, is used to determine the new values of the 605-GSG fields. Perhaps it would have been better to set the values of these fields closer to where the GVC file was validated.

Coincidental cohesion happens when functions are grouped together merely because they happen at the same time. A good example of this type of cohesion is the INITIALIZATION paragraph of a COBOL program.

```
A100-INITIALIZATION.
    OPEN INPUT    100-INPUT-FILE
         OUTPUT 200-OUTPUT-FILE.
    MOVE 'FVRASP01'              TO ABEND-PGMID
    MOVE 'VENDOR FILE UPDATE' TO ABEND-PGMNAME

    ACCEPT 350-CURRENT-YYMMDD FROM DATE
    ACCEPT 350-CURRENT-HHMMSS FROM TIME.
```

Here we have placed the opening of files, the initialization of some working storage fields, and the initialization of the date and time fields all in the same paragraph. There is no design reason for doing this, we just can't find a better place for these statements.

The type of coupling that modules have is often determined by the internal cohesion of the individual modules. Data coupling is often found when a module with sequential cohesion calls functionally cohesive modules. Both of the program rewrites that we have done are examples of this type of cohesion. Control coupling is often found among modules that exhibit procedural cohesion. We can see this in the example that we showed of procedural cohesion. Pathological coupling is found among modules that have temporal, logical, or coincidental cohesion.

If we use the concepts of coupling and cohesion as a measure of program structure, then a structured program is one that uses data coupling to unite modules that have functional, sequential, and communicational cohesion.

In the next chapters we will see a basic program structure that allows us to do this.

Chapter 4

The Structure of the Basic COBOL Program

In this chapter we will discuss the basic structure of a COBOL program. This may seem basic at first but bear with us. Some of the groundwork that we will be laying here will be important to the rest of our discussion.

COBOL (COmmon Business Oriented Language) was originally designed to be naturally suited to business data processing. The main features of a COBOL program are designed to allow a program to bring in a collection of records contained in a single file, or to combine the input of multiple files. The program will then uses these input files to repetitively manipulate the information on the records, to produce new or updated files, and to generate reports.

There are three levels of organization in a COBOL program. These three levels are paragraphs, which are the basic organization unit, sections which are a collection of paragraphs, and divisions which are a collection of sections. There are four divisions in every COBOL program, the Identification Division, the Environment Division, the Data Division, and the Procedure Division. The Identification Division is used to define the program to the operating system of the computer. An example of an Identification Division is shown as follows:

IDENTIFICATION DIVISION.

```
PROGRAM-ID.   PGMNAME.
AUTHOR.        EARL PARSONS.
DATE-WRITTEN. 11/11/92.
DATE-COMPILED.
```

In this division we specify such information as the eight character program name, the name of the person who wrote the program, the date the program was written. We can also add remarks that describe in English what the program does.

The Environment Division is used to describe how the program will function in relation to the operating system. This division consists of two sections; the Configuration Section which allows us to inform the operating system of any special needs that the program might have, and the Input-Output Section which allows us to inform the operating system of the files that the program expects to use.

```
ENVIRONMENT DIVISION.
CONFIGURATION SECTION.
INPUT-OUTPUT SECTION.
FILE-CONTROL.
     SELECT INPUT-FILE    ASSIGN TO UT-S-INPUT.
     SELECT REPORT-FILE   ASSIGN TO UT-S-REPORT.
```

These two divisions relate the program to the operating system. In the IBM mainframe environment, this relationship is controlled through IBM's Job Control Language (JCL). A sample of JCL is shown below.

```
//STEP01 EXEC PGM=PGMNAME
//STEPLIB  DD DSN=PROGRAM.LIBRARY,DISP=SHR
//INPUT    DD DSN=INPUT.FILE,DISP=SHR
//REPORT   DD SYSOUT=*
```

We will not take the time here for a discussion of the variations of JCL (there are other books on the subject). But from the above example we can see how the program and the JCL relate to each other. In the first JCL statement we designate the name of the program that we wish to execute. Note how the PGM= name (PGMNAME) is the same as the PROGRAM-NAME in the Identification Division of the program. In the second JCL statement, we designate the library where the program load module that is to be executed is stored.

In the third JCL statement we designate the name of the file that will be read in by the program. The data set name (DSN=) is the name of the file that the operating system knows the file by. The DD name (INPUT) is the same as the UT-S- name in the FILE-CONTROL section. This allows us to draw the following table.

UT-S-name	DD name	DSN name
UT-S-INPUT	//INPUT	DSN=INPUT.FILE

The fourth JCL statement is similar to the third, except that instead of pointing to a file name, this statement tells the operating system to send the report straight to a printer.

The Data Division is used to define the data storage fields that are used in the program. There are four sections in the data division. These are the File Section, the Working-Storage Section, the Linkage Section, and the Report Section.

In the File Section we define the characteristics and the layout of the input and output files. The file section entry for the Input File that we defined above is:

```
FD  INPUT-FILE
      BLOCK CONTAINS 0 RECORDS
      RECORD CONTAINS 80 CHARACTERS
      RECORDING MODE IS F
      LABEL RECORDS ARE STANDARD
      DATA RECORD IS INPUT-RECORD.
01  INPUT-RECORD    PIC X(80).
```

In this example, we should note that the name of the file (INPUT-FILE) corresponds to the name in the left hand side of the select statement. We should note that the record layout is defined by the field labeled INPUT-RECORD. We can also see that the expected record length is 80 bytes. This corresponds to the length that was specified in the record layout (INPUT-RECORD).

The Working-Storage Section defines the additional fields that are used by the program. We will discuss the details of working storage in chapter 5.

The Linkage Section is used to define the additional fields that this program shares with other programs. In COBOL, we have the ability to write small programs, which we then LINK together into one large module. The Linkage Section appears in the called program. In this Section the programmer designates which fields have been passed from the calling program to the called program.

The Report Section is used to define fields used by the special report writer that is available in the IBM COBOL compiler. Since this feature is not a supported in COBOL II, we will not discuss it in this text.

The Procedure Division contains the instructions that define the processing in the program. There are five types of statements in COBOL. The File Processing commands handle the external file interface between the program and the operating system. Assignment commands manipulates data and moves data from one field to another. Decision commands determine which process is going to be executed. Control commands determine which portion of the program is executed. Iterative commands cause the same process to be repeated a controlled number of times.

The basic file processing commands handle the interface between the program and the operating system. The OPEN command opens the named file for input or output processing. The CLOSE command closes the named file when processing is completed. The READ command brings data into the program from a file. The SORT and MERGE commands causes the records in a file (or a number of files) to be reordered. The RELEASE and RETURN commands move records in and out of the sort/merge processing. And the WRITE command moves data from the program to either a file or a report.

The basic assignment commands manipulate and move data. The ACCEPT command accepts data from the operating system, and copies it into a selected working storage field. The MOVE command copies the value of one field into another. The mathematical commands, ADD, ADD TO, ADD GIVING, COMPUTE, DIVIDE INTO, DIVIDE GIVING, MULTIPLY, SUBTRACT FROM and SUBTRACT GIVING, are used in equations to change the value of numeric data fields. The string processing commands EXAMINE, INSPECT, STRING, TRANSFORM, and UNSTRING, are used to manipulate a number of data fields at one time. And the array processing commands SEARCH and SET are used to find and manipulate data in an array.

The decision commands are used to determine which set of commands will be executed. These commands include the EVALUATE command, and the standard IF-THEN-ELSE structure.

Control commands control the order of processing within the program. The PERFORM command tells the program to execute the commands stored in another paragraph, and then come back to execute the next listed command after the PERFORM command. The GO TO command tells the program to do the commands in another paragraph. When this new paragraph is complete, control does not return to the next statement as it does in the PERFORM command. The go to paragraph must determine the new course. The EXIT command causes the execution of a paragraph to end. The CALL command starts the execution of another program which has been linked to our program. The ENTER command allows the use of several languages within a COBOL program. The GOBACK and STOP: causes the program to end.

Iterative commands include the PERFORM UNTIL, which causes a selected paragraph to be executed until a certain condition is met. On the other hand, the PERFORM VARYING causes a selected paragraph to continue to be executed while the value of a field is changed by the program.

These Procedure Division commands are in turn grouped into paragraphs and sections, which control the flow of processing through the program.

Sections in the procedure division were originally designed to help save CPU space in the older machines. Sections of the object module would be loaded into memory on Section boundaries. Thus code that would be processed together would be physically grouped together. The code within the sections would then be organized into paragraphs.

The development of faster CPUs and of MVS made the practice of designing programs around concurrent processing boundaries obsolete. The only requirements for section processing is found in programs which have an internal sort process. The input side and the output side of the sort will be in separate sections of the program.

The rest of the code in the procedure division is grouped into paragraphs. Each paragraph should, in turn, contain a unit of work. These units of work could be include functions to read the input file, write a report line, compute the commission amount, insert a database record, or edit an input field. The level of structure in the program is determined by how well these units of work are defined (cohesion), and how they are linked together (coupling). We can represent the basic organization of a COBOL program with the following "Structure Chart."

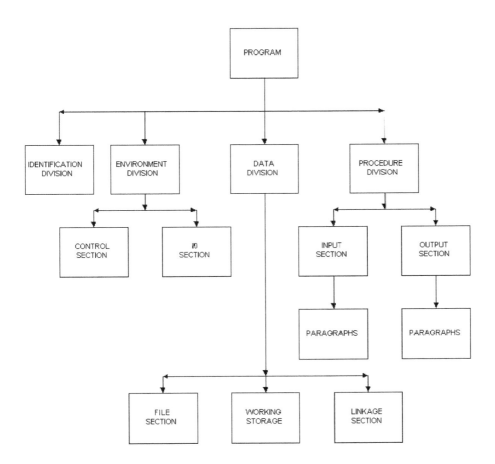

Figure 4.1

The purpose of a Structure Chart is to show the hierarchical structure of a program. Each level on the chart shows a subordinate level of control. For example, the chart clearly shows that the CONTROL SECTION and the I/O SECTION are subordinate to the ENVIRONMENT DIVISION.

The example also shows one of the major disadvantages of a structure chart in that they are hard to draw and harder to maintain. As you can see, the subordinate modules from the DATA DIVISION are shown under the other modules of the same level because this is the only way the chart will fit on the page. Additionally, if the REPORT SECTION were to be moved from the DATA DIVISION to the PROCEDURE DIVISION, we would have to redraw a large portion of the chart.

To remedy this situation, we will modify the design of the basic structure chart by turning it 90 degrees, and calling it a Cascade Structure Chart, or Cascade Chart (because I am tired of typing the word "structure".) This new chart will appear as follows:

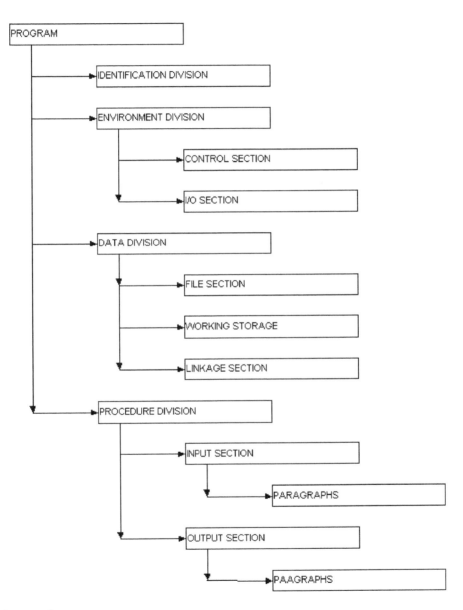

Figure 4.2

We can see that this type of chart is easier to draw and to maintain. As we can see, each hierarchical level is displayed in the same horizontal position. This allows us to have an infinite number of modules under a single heading without having to worry about wrapping around the page. Also, when we move a module from one area to another is a simple matter of deleting a line and inserting it somewhere else. We should also note that through the proper use of indentations, even the arrows can be eliminated.

We can also see that this structure is more closely aligned with the way that programs are actually written. Thus the chart could serve not only as a model of the program, but as the basis for both the prototype and the actual program. We will be using these Cascade Diagrams throughout the rest of this text.

In the next chapter we will use coupling and cohesion, and a cascade diagram, to show how to organize the working storage portion of the program.

Chapter 5

Structuring the Data Division

Before we look at the procedure division which contains the instructions to manipulate data, we need to understand how the data is organized and defined. When a COBOL program runs, it is assigned an area of the computer's main memory in which to store values. This memory area is sub divided by the program into fields. The definition of each of these fields contains the beginning address of the field, the length of the field, and the format of the data (Display, Computational, Binary, etc). When we reference a field in a COBOL program we are accessing a specific area (beginning address and length) of the machine's memory.

We use the data division to control the definition of these fields. As we stated in chapter four, the data division is divided into four sections. These sections are the FILE SECTION, the WORKING-STORAGE SECTION, the LINKAGE SECTION. The data areas in these sections are defined with a command that contains the:

1) level number.
2) field name.
3) type of field.
4) length of the field.
5) type of field organization that is used.
6) any specific initial value.

For example, the following command defines the listed field attributes:

01 FIELD-NAME-1   PICTURE X(09) VALUE 'ABCDEFGHI'.

1) level number of 01.
2) field name of FIELD-NAME-1.
3) type of field of X, for alphanumeric.
4) length of the field of 9 bytes.
5) field organization type of display.
6) an initial value of ABCDEFGHI.

The level number controls the organization of the field definitions. There are two types of field definitions. The elementary field definition defines a specific area. The compound field definition is a collection of elementary field definitions. To continue our example:

01 FIELD-NAME-1.
    05 FIELD-NAME-2   PIC X(05) VALUE 'ABCDE'.
    05 FIELD-NAME-3   PIC X(04) VALUE 'FGHI'.

FIELD-NAME-2 and FIELD-NAME-3 are elementary fields. FIELD-NAME-1 is a compound field. We can also see that this structure allows us two different ways to address the same area of computer memory. We can draw a map of this data structure as follows:

A	B	C	D	E	F	G	H	I
		<-----		FIELD-NAME-1		---->		
<-----		FIELD-NAME-2		---->	<-----		FIELD-NAME-3	---->

In this example we can see two different ways to reference the same 9 bytes of memory. We can refer to all ten bytes of memory by using the field named FIELD-NAME-1. Accessing this field gives us the value

"ABCDEFGHI". We can also refer to one of two subsections of the larger field. FIELD-NAME-2 contains the value "ABCDE", and FIELD-NAME-3 contains the value "FGHI". We can continue to split these field definitions until we are defining each byte. We simply increment the level number for each new level.

```
01  FIELD-NAME-1.
    05  FIELD-NAME-2        PIC X(05).
    05  FIELD-NAME-3.
        07  FIELD-NAME-4    PIC X(02).
        07  FIELD-NAME-5.
            09  FIELD-NAME-6 PIC X(01).
            09  FIELD-NAME-7 PIC X(01).
```

The level number can be any value from 01 to 99, although the values of 77 and 88 have a special meaning which we will not discuss here. We usually increment the level number by two to simplify future changes to the program. This way, if we want to insert a new level, we could give it an even level number, and save ourselves from having to change all of the subsequent level numbers.

The 01 level also has a special meaning. The computer internally refers to its main memory in blocks of eight bytes. Each group of 8 bytes is called a "full word". The beginning memory address of an 01 level field is always placed at the first byte of a full word (often referred to as "the full word boundary"). The problem with this is that a series of 01 level fields can leave unused bytes between the fields. For example, the field definitions:

```
01  FIELD-NAME-1    PIC X(06) VALUE 'ABCEDF'.
01  FIELD-NAME-2    PIC X(05) VALUE 'HIJKL'.
01  FIELD-NAME-3    PIC X(04) VALUE 'NOPQ'.
```

would appear in memory as:

FIELD NAME	LAYOUT OF A FULL WORD IN MEMORY							
FIELD-NAME-1	A	B	C	D	E	F		
FIELD-NAME-2	H	I	J	K	L			
FIELD-NAME-3	N	O	P	Q				

We can see that this definition wastes 9 bytes of memory storage (the cross hatched parts of the table. There are two ways to avoid this waste. In the first method we can group the three fields under the same 01 level.

```
01  FIELD-GROUP.
      05  FIELD-NAME-1    PIC X(06) VALUE 'ABCEDF'.
      05  FIELD-NAME-2    PIC X(05) VALUE 'HIJKL'.
      05  FIELD-NAME-3    PIC X(04) VALUE 'NOPQ'.
```

This will cause the operating system to string the fields together in memory.

FIELD NAME	LAYOUT OF A FULL WORD IN MEMORY							
FIELD-GROUP	A	B	C	D	E	F	H	I
FIELD-NAME-2	J	K	L	M	N			

By doing this we save 8 bytes of memory space by eliminating the need for the third memory word. We also only have three bytes of allocated but unused space. In the second method we can define the fields with a level number of 77. These fields are strung together in the same manner as the elementary fields under the single 01 level FIELD-GROUP.

```
77  FIELD-NAME-1    PIC X(06) VALUE 'ABCEDF'.
77  FIELD-NAME-2    PIC X(05) VALUE 'HIJKL'.
77  FIELD-NAME-3    PIC X(04) VALUE 'NOPQ'.
```

The advantage of grouping fields under a single 01 level, rather than a long list of 77 levels, is that we can use this feature to help organize the program. The data division sections can have paragraphs, just as the procedure division sections are organized into paragraphs. We can think of each of these paragraphs as an 01 level and its subordinate fields. (We should even note that both the 01 level and a procedure division paragraph name start in column 8, while the subordinate fields, and procedure division statements both start in column 12.)

This realization allows us to apply the rules of coupling and cohesion to paragraph allocation. We can group data division definitions into one of several categories:

1) input file descriptions.

2) output file descriptions.

3) those working storage field definitions that we see in nearly every program. Examples of these fields include process control flags; input, output, and process counters; date and time conversion fields; and process break fields.

4) those working storage field definitions that are unique to a particular program. Examples of these could include computational hold fields and data conversion fields.

5) report layout definitions.

6) tables and arrays.

7) working storage input and output file layout definitions.

And we can add this detail to our Cascade Chart from chapter four.

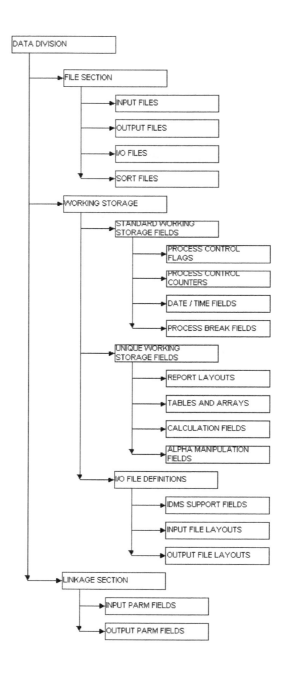

Figure 5.1

By doing this we make each 01 level of working storage fields function-ally cohesive.

We can also assign a numeric prefix to each field in the data division to identify which group it belongs to. A suggested set of prefixes is:

100- Input file descriptions (FDs in the Data Division).
200- Output file descriptions (FDs in the Data Division).
300- Standard Working Storage fields.
310- Process control flags
320- Process control counters.
330- Date and time conversion fields.
340- Process break fields.
400- Unique working storage fields.
600- Report layout definitions.
800- Tables and arrays.
900- Input and output file layout definitions.
999- Linkage Section fields

We will see the use of the 500- prefix for another chapter. We have also reserved the 700- prefix for additional report layouts.

Under this scheme, we can also use the second position to identify mul-tiple occurrences of the same item. For example, if we have two reports in the same program, then fields belonging to the first report would be num-bered 610-, and the second would be numbered 620-. We can further break this down, where fields belonging to the first line of the first report would be numbered 611-, and fields belonging to the second line would be numbered 612-.

We can see this organization in the example below, which is the Working Storage of a program that :

1) reads in an input file containing sales records.

2) reports on each input record.

3) writes out a file showing sales commissions.

4) reports control totals showing the input and output record counts.

```
DATA-DIVISION.
FILE-SECTION.
FD  100-INPUT-FILE
    BLOCK CONTAINS 0 RECORDS
    RECORD CONTAINS 80 CHARACTERS
    RECORDING MODE IS F
    LABEL RECORDS ARE STANDARD
    DATA RECORD IS 100-INPUT-RECORD.
01  100-INPUT-RECORD     PIC X(80).

FD  200-OUTPUT-FILE
    BLOCK CONTAINS 0 RECORDS
    RECORD CONTAINS 80 CHARACTERS
    RECORDING MODE IS F
    LABEL RECORDS ARE STANDARD
    DATA RECORD IS 200-OUTPUT-RECORD.
01  200-OUTPUT-RECORD     PIC X(80).

FD  210-REPORT-FILE
    BLOCK CONTAINS 0 RECORDS
    RECORD CONTAINS 133 CHARACTERS
    RECORDING MODE IS F
    LABEL RECORDS ARE STANDARD
    DATA RECORD IS 210-REPORT-RECORD.
01  210-REPORT-RECORD   PIC X(133).

WORKING-STORAGE SECTION.
01 310-CONTROL-FLAGS.
   05 310-END-OF-FILE-FLAG    PIC X(01) VALUE 'N'.

01 320-CONTROL-COUNTERS.
   05 320-RECORDS-READ       PIC 9(05) COMP-3 VALUE ZEROES.
   05 320-RECORDS-WRITTEN    PIC 9(05) COMP-3 VALUE ZEROES.
```

```
01 330-DATE-CONTROL-AREA.
   05 330-CURRENT-CCYYMMDD.
      07 330-CURRENT-CC        PIC X(02) VALUE SPACES.
      07 330-CURRENT-YYMMDD.
         09  330-CURRENT-YY    PIC X(02) VALUE SPACES.
         09  330-CURRENT-MM    PIC X(02) VALUE SPACES.
         09  330-CURRENT-DD    PIC X(02) VALUE SPACES.
   05 330-CURRENT-HHMMSS.
      09 330-CURRENT-HH        PIC X(02) VALUE SPACES.
      09 330-CURRENT-MM        PIC X(02) VALUE SPACES.
      09 330-CURRENT-SS        PIC X(02) VALUE SPACES.
```

```
*********************************************************************************
*** THESE FIELDS ARE USED IN THE COMMISSION AMOUNT CALCUALTION***
*********************************************************************************

01 400-UNIQUE-FIELDS.
   05  400-COMMISSION-PERCENT  PIC 9(02)     COMP-3 VALUE 10.
   05  400-COMMISSION-AMOUNT   PIC 9(05)V99 COMP-3 VALUE ZEROES.
   05  400-SALES-AMT           PIC 9(05)V99 COMP-3 VALUE ZEROES.
```

```
*********************************************************************************
*** THIS AREA IS USED TO DEFINE THE COMMISSION REPORT        ***
*********************************************************************************

01 610-SALES-REPORT.
   05 610-FIRST-USAGE          PIC X(02)              VALUE 'Y'.
   05 610-LINE-COUNT           PIC 9(02) COMP-3 VALUE 77.
   05 610-LINE-LIMIT           PIC 9(02) COMP-3 VALUE 60.
   05 610-PAGE-COUNTER         PIC 9(05) COMP-3 VALUE ZEROES.
   05 611-HEADER-LINE.
      07 FILLER                PIC X(01) VALUE SPACES.
      07 FILLER                PIC X(08) VALUE 'PROGRAM1'.
      07 FILLER                PIC X(25) VALUE SPACES.
      07 611-HEADER-LITERAL    PIC X(30) VALUE SPACES.
      07 FILLER                PIC X(15) VALUE SPACES.
      07 611-CURRENT-DATE.
         09 611-CURRENT-MM     PIC X(02) VALUE SPACES.
         09 FILLER             PIC X(01) VALUE '/'.
         09 611-CURRENT-DD     PIC X(02) VALUE SPACES.
         09 FILLER             PIC X(01) VALUE '/'.
         09 611-CURRENT-YY     PIC X(02) VALUE SPACES.
```

```
          07  FILLER                PIC X(03) VALUE SPACES.
          07  FILLER                PIC X(05) VALUE 'PAGE'.
          07  611-PAGE-NUMBER       PIC ZZZZ9 VALUE ZEROES.

      05  614-DETAIL-HEADER.
          07  FILLER                PIC X(05)    VALUE SPACES.
          07  FILLER                PIC X(05)    VALUE 'EMPNO'.
          07  FILLER                PIC X(01)    VALUE SPACES.
          07  FILLER                PIC X(07)    VALUE 'CATALOG'.
          07  FILLER                PIC X(02)    VALUE SPACES.
          07  FILLER                PIC X(07)    VALUE ' PRICE'.
          07  FILLER                PIC X(02)    VALUE SPACES.
          07  FILLER                PIC X(05)    VALUE 'QUANT'.
          07  FILLER                PIC X(02)    VALUE SPACES.
          07  FILLER                PIC X(08)    VALUE 'TOT SALE'.
          07  FILLER                PIC X(02)    VALUE SPACES.
          07  FILLER                PIC X(08)    VALUE 'COMM AMT'.

      05  615-DETAIL-LINE.
          07  FILLER                PIC X(05)    VALUE SPACES.
          07  615-EMPLOYEE-NBR      PIC X(05)    VALUE SPACES.
          07  FILLER                PIC X(02)    VALUE SPACES.
          07  615-CATALOG-NBR       PIC X(06)    VALUE SPACES.
          07  FILLER                PIC X(02)    VALUE SPACES.
          07  615-UNIT-PRICE        PIC ZZZ9V99  VALUE ZEROES.
          07  FILLER                PIC X(02)    VALUE SPACES.
          07  615-NUMBER-SOLD       PIC ZZZZ9    VALUE ZEROES.
          07  FILLER                PIC X(02)    VALUE SPACES.
          07  615-SALES-AMT         PIC ZZZZ9V99 VALUE ZEROES.
          07  FILLER                PIC X(02)    VALUE SPACES.
          07  615-COMMISSION-AMT    PIC ZZZZ9V99 VALUE ZEROES.

  ************************************************************************************
  *** AREA DEFINES THE CONTROL REPORT                                             ***
  ************************************************************************************
  01  620-CONTROL-REPORT.
      05  620-LINE-COUNT            PIC 9(02) COMP-3 VALUE 77.
      05  620-LINE-LIMIT            PIC 9(02) COMP-3 VALUE 60.
      05  620-PAGE-COUNTER          PIC 9(05) COMP-3 VALUE ZEROES.
      05  621-CONTROL-LINE.
```

```
      07  FILLER                    PIC X(01) VALUE SPACES.
      07  621-CONTROL-DESC          PIC X(20) VALUE SPACES.
      07  FILLER                    PIC X(01) VALUE SPACES.
      07  621-CONTROL-AMT           PIC ZZZZ9 VALUE ZEROES.


01  690-BLANK-LINE            PIC X(05) VALUE SPACES.


****************************************************************************
*** AREA DEFINES THE INPUT FILE LAYOUT                               ***
****************************************************************************
01  910-INPUT-FILE-AREA.
      05  910-EMPLOYEE-NBR     PIC X(05)    VALUE SPACES.
      05  910-CATALOG-NBR      PIC X(06)    VALUE SPACES.
      05  910-UNIT-PRICE       PIC 9(04)V99 VALUE ZEROES.
      05  910-NUMBER-SOLD      PIC 9(05)    VALUE ZEROES.
      05  910-TOTAL-SALES      PIC 9(05)V99 VALUE ZEROES.


****************************************************************************
*** AREA DEFINES THE OUTPUT FILE LAYOUT                              ***
****************************************************************************
01  920-OUTPUT-FILE-AREA.
      05  920-EMPLOYEE-NBR     PIC X(05)    VALUE SPACES.
      05  920-COMMISSION-AMT   PIC 9(05)V99 VALUE ZEROES.
```

We can see another benefit of the numbering scheme is the ability to simplify and unite field names. The field name EMPLOYEE-NBR is used three times; in the input file area, the report layout, and in the output file area. We also have plans later in the book to use this field name in other definitions. Using the numeric prefixes makes each occurrence unique to the compiler, while keeping the actual name the same. Without the prefixes, we would have to spell each occurrence differently. This can cause a great deal of confusion when we build programs with hundreds of names.

We should also note a number of other techniques that we used to improve the readability and the maintainability of the program. First, we have separated the FD definitions from the input (910) and the output (920) file layout definitions. We did this so that we could isolate the FD definitions. It is easier to see the relationship between the SELECT statements and the FDs after we clear away the layout definitions.

Second, we should note that there is a one to one relationship between the fields in the detail report line, and the fields in the detail report header line. This allows for easier changes because we are dealing with individual fields, instead of trying to match the displacement of the field in the report line.

Third, we have assigned an initial value to each field in working storage. If the initial value is not assigned the field will retain the value from the last use of that field. Since we cannot control what the last program did with that area of memory, it is important that we initialize each field. This initialization can be done either in the working storage definitions or with move statements in the beginning of the program. From a cohesion standpoint, we feel that it is better to do this initialization at the time the field is defined.

For the fourth technique we have been careful with the alignment of the definitions on the page. Neat code is easier to read and understand. We have also found that many small mistakes, (such as misspellings, missing periods, and incorrect level numbers) are easier to spot because they "stick out like a sore thumb".

Using these techniques allows us to structure the working storage portion of the program. We can see that the individual groups of code are functionally cohesive, and that the 01 levels are sequentially cohesive. This makes the Working Storage area easier to change and to maintain. In the next chapter we will build the basic program that uses this working storage.

Chapter 6

The Design of the Basic COBOL Program

A friend of mine, when learning that I had been writing COBOL programs for 20 years, asked "When are you going to write your second program?" While I hope he was kidding me, he did hit upon a basic truth. For all of the millions of COBOL programs that are currently in production, only a small portion of each program is unique.

The problem is that this redundancy is not readily apparent. There are as many different programming styles as there are programmers. There may even be more styles than programmers, because many programmers start from scratch with each new assignment.

When we look at a COBOL program, we can divide the procedure code functions into two major classifications. The first classification is housekeeping and overhead. These are the basic functions that we find in most programs and such as data retrieval, and user presentation. This includes, file opening and closing, file input and output, report control, program initialization, counter control, database and screen processing, etc. The second classification is data manipulation, which is defined by the business rules that govern the function of the program. These are the functions that are unique to this program. This includes arithmetic manipulation, moving data to output files and reports, table searches, data validation, etc. This classification can be made by asking the question,

"Would a change to a business rule for this program directly effect this function?" A change to the layout of an output file would effect the paragraph that loads the output record. But this same change would not effect the process to write the record to the output file.

In most programs, these functions are mixed together. This makes finding the specific data manipulation functions as difficult as panning for gold. You have to sift through a lot of sand to find the nugget that you are looking for. This often requires the programmer to study the entire program to understand or debug a single function.

But what if there were a way to isolate the data manipulation functions from the overhead functions, and then standardize the way the overhead functions were written. The first advantage to doing this is that we can reduce debugging time because we would only have to read and small portion of each program to understand it's function. The second advantage is that we can reduce the amount of code we actually have to develop and debug, because we would use the same already tested and proven functions over and over again.

In this chapter we will develop a basic program that will show how to split the housekeeping functions from the data manipulation functions. The example we will build will be a continuation of program that we built the Working Storage for in Chapter 4. Again this program will read records from an input file, report on each input record, write out a file showing sales commissions, and report control totals showing input and output record counts.

A basic COBOL program has three elements. The first element is the initialization process. This process includes these functions which are done once to prepare for the main processing. These functions include setting the initial value of working, obtaining date and time values from the operating system, and opening files.

The second element is the main the repetitive process. This is the main process of the program, which is done once for each "unit of work". A unit of work consists of everything that is done for a particular transaction. In our example, the unit of work is reading the input record, writing a report line, writing an output line. This unit of work is repeated for every input record.

The third element is termination. These are functions that are done once when the main process in complete. This functions include writing of summary reports, closing files, and telling the operating system to terminate the program.

We can then add this information to our Cascade Chart from Chapter 3.

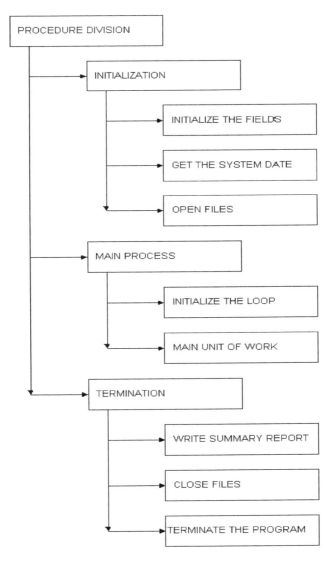

Figure 6.1

This structure gives us three Functionally Cohesive modules, which we can control with a Sequentially Cohesive Module. Translating this structure into COBOL code gives us the following results:

```
PROCEDURE DIVISION.
    PERFORM INITIALIZATION.
    PERFORM MAIN-PROCESS
    PERFORM TERMINATION.

MAIN-PROCESS.
    PERFORM INITIALIZE-LOOP
    PERFORM UNTIL END-OF-PROCESS
        PERFORM UNIT-OF-WORK
    END-PERFORM.
```

Applying this structure to our example program gives us the following code fragment:

```
PROCEDURE DIVISION.
    PERFORM INITIALIZATION.
    PERFORM MAIN-PROCESS
    PERFORM TERMINATION.

MAIN-PROCESS.
    PERFORM READ-INPUT-RECORD.
    PERFORM UNTIL 310-END-OF-FILE-FLAG = 'Y'
        PERFORM WRITE-REPORT-LINE
        PERFORM WRITE-OUTPUT-LINE
        PERFORM READ-INPUT-RECORD
    END-PERFORM.
```

When we build PERFORM UNTIL loops, it is also best if we initialize the loop, and then put the driving function at the bottom of the performed paragraph. Otherwise, we would have to build it like this:

```
MAIN-PROCESS.
    PERFORM UNTIL 310-END-OF-FILE-FLAG = 'Y'
        PERFORM READ-INPUT-RECORD
        IF 310-END-OF-FILE-FLAG = 'N'
            PERFORM WRITE-REPORT-LINE
            PERFORM WRITE-OUTPUT-LINE
        END-IF.
    END-PERFORM.
```

This second process has us checking for the end of file condition twice. Once by the PERFORM UNTIL, and the second time inside the MAIN-PROCESS paragraph with the IF statement. We should also note that the two WRITE paragraphs can be parsed into smaller functions. Doing this gives us the following new main paragraph:

```
MAIN-PROCESS.
    PERFORM READ-INPUT-RECORD.
    PERFORM UNTIL 310-END-OF-FILE-FLAG = 'Y'
        PERFORM COMPUTE-COMMISSION
        PERFORM LOAD-REPORT-LINE
        PERFORM CHECK-REPORT-HDR
        PERFORM WRITE-REPORT-LINE
        PERFORM LOAD-OUTPUT-RECORD
        PERFORM WRITE-OUTPUT-RECORD
        PERFORM READ-INPUT-RECORD
    END-PERFORM.
```

Each of these paragraphs are functionally cohesive, because they execute a single function, or a single unit of work. The COMPUTE-COMMISSION paragraph computes the commission amount for each input record. The LOAD-REPORT-LINE paragraph populates the report line fields with data from the input record, and the commission amount. The CHECK-REPORT-HDR paragraph checks the line counter to see if the program needs to advance to the next page. If it does, the paragraph will write the page header for the next page. The WRITE-REPORT-LINE paragraph writes the report detail line, incrementing the line counter. The LOAD-OUTPUT-RECORD paragraph populates the output record fields with data from the input record, and the commission amount. The WRITE-OUTPUT-RECORD paragraph writes the output record to the output file, and increments the counter. The READ-INPUT-RECORD paragraph reads the input record from the input file, checks for end of file, and increments the counter.

We can then designate which paragraph in MAIN-PROCESS are overhead, and which do data manipulation. The overhead paragraphs include CHECK-REPORT-HDR, WRITE-REPORT-LINE, WRITE-OUTPUT-RECORD, and READ-INPUT-RECORD. Each of these functions are common to most COBOL programs, and not specific to the unit of work that the program is trying to process. The data manipulation paragraphs include COMPUTE-COMMISSION, LOAD-REPORT-LINE, and LOAD-OUTPUT-RECORD. Each of these paragraphs would be effected if the unit of work is changed.

To make the program easier to read, we will move the overhead paragraphs to the bottom of the program, and we will cluster the data manipulation paragraphs together. To encourage this grouping, we can assign standard prefixes to the paragraph names in the same way that we assigned prefixes to the working storage definitions. Each prefix consists of a letter code that designates which type of paragraph it is, and a three digit number code that shows the paragraphs position in the hierarchy. The basic letter codes that we will use are as follows:

A—Initialization.
B—Main Unit of Work.
C—Secondary Unit of Work.
D—Paragraphs that are used by more than one function.
E—Termination.
X—File Input and Output processing.
Y—Report Processing.
Z – Abend

This allows us to label the paragraphs of our basic program as follows:

```
PROCEDURE DIVISION.
      PERFORM A000-INITIALIZATION.
      PERFORM B000-MAIN-PROCESS
      PERFORM E000-TERMINATION.

B000-MAIN-PROCESS.
    PERFORM X100-READ-INPUT-RECORD.
    PERFORM UNTIL 310-END-OF-FILE-FLAG = 'Y'
        PERFORM B200-COMPUTE-COMMISSION
        PERFORM B400-LOAD-REPORT-LINE
        PERFORM Y100-WRITE-REPORT-LINE
        PERFORM B500-LOAD-OUTPUT-RECORD
        PERFORM X200-WRITE-OUTPUT-RECORD
        PERFORM X100-READ-INPUT-RECORD
    END-PERFORM.

B200-COMPUTE-COMMISSION.

B400-LOAD-REPORT-LINE.

B500-LOAD-OUTPUT-RECORD.

E000-TERMINATION.

X100-READ-NEXT-RECORD.

X200-WRITE-OUTPUT-RECORD.

Y100-WRITE-REPORT-LINE.
      PERFORM Y110-CHECK-RPT-HDR.

Y110-CHECK-RPT-HDR.
```

This example gives us cleaner code for three reasons. First, the house-keeping functions have been separated from the main functions. Second, we can easily trace the execution path in the main functions by looking at the prefix of each paragraph. And third, each paragraph is a separate module, executing a single unit of work.

Now that we have built the basic program structure, we can look at each of the individual function paragraphs.

```
*****************************************************************************************
*** PARAGRAPH PERFORMS PROGRAM INITIALIZATION. THIS        ***
*** INCLUDES: OPENING OF THE FILES                         ***
***           OBTAINING THE CURRENT DATE AND TIME          ***
*****************************************************************************************
A000-INITIALIZATION.
      OPEN INPUT   100-INPUT-FILE
           OUTPUT 200-OUTPUT-FILE
                  210-REPORT-FILE.
      ACCEPT 330-CURRENT-YYMMDD FROM DATE.
      ACCEPT 330-CURRENT-HHMMSS FROM TIME-OF-DAY.
```

We have now opened the files for processing. We have also loaded the current date and time into working storage fields. The date is in the year (last 2 digits), month, and day formats. The time is in the hour (military time), minute, and second format.

```
*****************************************************************************************
*** PARAGRAPH COMPUTES THE SALESMANS COMMISSION. THE       ***
*** COMMISSION IS COMPUTED AS A PERCENTAGE OF THE TOTAL     ***
*** SALES.                                                 ***
*****************************************************************************************
B200-COMPUTE-COMMISSION
      COMPUTE 400-SALES-AMT = 900-UNIT-PRICE
                     * 900-NUMBER-SOLD.
      COMPUTE ROUNDED 400-COMMISSION-AMT
                 = 400-SALES-AMT
                 / 400-COMMISSION-PERCENT.
```

Here we have used compute statements to determine the salesman's commission. We did this in two steps to improve the cohesion of the statements in the paragraph. This also makes the debugging process easier, by allowing us to examine (if necessary) the process on a step by step basis.

```
******************************************************************************
*** PARAGRAPH LOADS THE OUTPUT REPORT LINE.                              ***
******************************************************************************
B400-LOAD-REPORT-LINE.
        MOVE 910-EMPLOYEE-NBR      TO 615-EMPLOYEE-NBR.
        MOVE 910-CATALOG-NBR       TO 615-CATALOG-NBR.
        MOVE 910-UNIT-PRICE        TO 615-UNIT-PRICE.
        MOVE 910-NUMBER-SOLD       TO 615-NUMBER-SOLD.
        MOVE 400-SALES-AMT         TO 615-SALES-AMT.
        MOVE 400-COMMISSION-AMT TO 615-COMMISSION-AMT.


******************************************************************************
*** PARAGRAPH LOADS THE OUTPUT REPORT LINE.                              ***
******************************************************************************
B500-LOAD-OUTPUT-RECORD.
        MOVE 910-EMPLOYEE-NBR      TO 920-EMPLOYEE-NBR.
        MOVE 400-COMMISSION-AMT TO 920-COMMISSION-AMT.
```

These paragraphs load the output file and output record. Please note how the use of the prefix numbers on the fields as aids in understanding the source of each value, without having to search through the entire working storage of the program:

1) the 910- fields are from the input file.
2) the 400- fields are computed inside the program.

```
******************************************************************************
*** PARAGRAPH CALLS THE PARAGRAPH THAT WRITES THE CONTROL ***
*** REPORT PAGE, AND THEN CLOSES THE FILES.                       ***
******************************************************************************
E000-TERMINATION.
        PERFORM E100-CONTROL-REPORT.
        CLOSE 100-INPUT-FILE
                200-OUTPUT-FILE
                210-REPORT-FILE.
        GOBACK.
```

This paragraph serves as a gateway to the conclusion of processing. Here we call the control report processing, close the files, and issue a GOBACK command.

```
*****************************************************************************
*** PARAGRAPH WRITES THE STATISTICAL REPORT LINES              ***
*****************************************************************************
E100-CONTROL-REPORT.
     MOVE 'RECORDS READ'        TO 621-CONTROL-DESC
     MOVE 320-RECORDS-READ      TO 621-CONTROL-COUNTER
     PERFORM Y300-WRITE-CONTROL-LINE.

     MOVE 'RECORDS WRITTEN'     TO 621-CONTROL-DESC
     MOVE 320-RECORDS-WRITTEN TO 621-CONTROL-COUNTER
     PERFORM Y300-WRITE-CONTROL-LINE.
```

We have separated the unique functions (loading the output fields) from the standard writing of the report lines.

```
*****************************************************************************
*** PARAGRAPH READS IN THE INPUT FILE RECORDS SEQUENTIALLY***
*****************************************************************************
X100-READ-INPUT-FILE.
     READ 100-INPUT-FILE INTO 910-INPUT-FILE-AREA
       AT END MOVE 'Y' TO 310-END-OF-FILE-FLAG.

     IF 310-END-OF-FILE-FLAG = 'N'
       ADD 1 TO 320-RECORDS-READ.
```

In this paragraph, we read the input file into the working storage definition area. When the read command senses that there are no more records left in the input file, then it will return the at end signal to the program. At this point the program will set the END-OF-FILE-FLAG to the value of 'Y'. If the end of file flag is 'N' then we will increment the control counter 320-RECORDS-READ.

We could have also written this function using the special 88 level field definitions. For example, we could have built the following definition:

```
01 310-CONTROL-FLAGS.
    05 310-END-OF-FILE-FLAG    PIC X(01) VALUE 'N'.
    88 310-END-OF-FILE                   VALUE 'Y'.
```

then the read paragraph would have been written as:

```
X100-READ-INPUT-FILE.
    READ 100-INPUT-FILE INTO 900-INPUT-FILE-AREA
        AT END MOVE 'Y' TO 310-END-OF-FILE-FLAG.

    IF 310-END-OF-FILE
        ADD 1 TO 320-RECORDS-READ.
```

Note how we used the condition instead of checking the value of the field with an equals sign. The real value of conditions comes when a field can have multiple true values. For example, the definition of valid month abbreviations:

```
01 410-VALID-MONTH-CHECK PIC X(03) VALUE SPACES..
    88 410-VALID-MONTH  VALUE 'JAN' 'FEB' 'MAR' 'APR'
                              'MAY' 'JUN' 'JLY' 'AUG'
                              'SEP' 'OCT' 'NOV' 'DEC'.
```

uses the single if statement:

```
    IF 410-VALID-MONTH
```

instead of a compound IF statement with 11 ORs.

```
*********************************************************************************
*** PARAGRAPH WRITES THE DETAIL RECORD TO THE OUTPUT FILE***
*********************************************************************************
```

```
X200-WRITE-OUTPUT-RECORD.
     WRITE 200-OUTPUT-REC FROM 920-OUTPUT-FILE-AREA.
     ADD 1 TO 320-RECORDS-WRITTEN.
```

In this paragraph we write the output file record from the 910- area. Note that we only use the AFTER ADVANCING clause when we are writing a report and we need a carriage control character for the printer to work correctly.

```
***************************************************************************************
*** PARAGRAPH WRITES OUT THE DETAIL LINE TO THE REPORT      ***
*** AFTER IT CHECKS THE LINE COUNT AGAINST THE LINE SIZE     ***
***************************************************************************************
Y100-WRITE-REPORT-LINE.
     ADD 1 TO 610-LINE-COUNTER.
     IF 610-LINE-COUNTER GREATER THAN 610-LINE-LIMIT
        PERFORM Y110-WRITE-PAGE-HEADER.
     WRITE 210-REPORT-REC FROM 615-DETAIL-LINE
        AFTER ADVANCING 1 LINES.


***************************************************************************************
*** PARAGRAPH WRITES OUT THE REPORT HEADER AFTER             ***
*** INCREMENTING THE PAGE COUNTER, AND IF NECCESARY          ***
*** SETTING THE DATE AND HEADER LITERALS.                    ***
***************************************************************************************
Y110-WRITE-PAGE-HEADER.
     IF 610-FIRST-USAGE = 'Y'
        MOVE 'N' TO 610-FIRST-USAGE
        MOVE 'COMMISSION SALES REPORT' TO 611-HEADER-LITERAL
        MOVE 330-CURRENT-YY          TO 611-CURRENT-YY
        MOVE 330-CURRENT-MM          TO 611-CURRENT-MM
        MOVE 330-CURRENT-DD          TO 611-CURRENT-DD.
     ADD 1                            TO 610-PAGE-COUNTER
     MOVE 610-PAGE-COUNTER            TO 611-PAGE-NUMBER
     MOVE 4                           TO 610-LINE-COUNTER.
```

```
WRITE 210-REPORT-REC FROM 611-HEADER-LINE
    AFTER ADVANCING PAGE.
WRITE 210-REPORT-REC FROM 614-DETAIL-HEADER
    AFTER ADVANCING 1 LINES.
WRITE 210-REPORT-REC FROM 690-BLANK-LINE
    AFTER ADVANCING 1 LINES.
```

We have concentrated all of the overhead to write a report in these paragraphs. We first check the line counter, and if it is greater than the limit (which it is on the first write) then we will execute the paragraph that builds the header lines. Here we again check the initial value of the 610-FIRST-USAGE switch, to see if we need to load the report date and header.

```
****************************************************************************
***  PARAGRAPH WRITES OUT THE CONTROL REPORT RECORDS AFTER***
***  IT CHECKS THE LINE COUNTER.                                        ***
****************************************************************************
Y300-WRITE-CONTROL-LINE.
    ADD 1 TO 620-LINE-COUNTER.
    IF   610-LINE-COUNTER GREATER THAN 610-LINE-LIMIT
        PERFORM Y110-WRITE-PAGE-HEADER.
    WRITE 210-REPORT-REC FROM 615-DETAIL-LINE
        AFTER ADVANCING 1 LINES.


****************************************************************************
***  PARAGRAPH WRITES OUT THE REPORT HEADER AFTER          ***
***  INCREMENTING THE PAGE COUNTER, AND IF NECCESARY       ***
***  SETTING THE DATE AND HEADER LITERALS.                 ***
****************************************************************************
Y110-WRITE-PAGE-HEADER.
    MOVE 'COMMISSION SALES REPORT'   TO 611-HEADER-LITERAL
    MOVE 330-CURRENT-YY              TO 611-CURRENT-YY
    MOVE 330-CURRENT-MM              TO 611-CURRENT-MM
    MOVE 330-CURRENT-DD              TO 611-CURRENT-DD.
    ADD 1                            TO 610-PAGE-COUNTER
    MOVE 610-PAGE-COUNTER            TO 611-PAGE-NUMBER
    MOVE 4                           TO 610-LINE-COUNTER.
```

```
WRITE 210-REPORT-REC FROM 611-HEADER-LINE
    AFTER ADVANCING PAGE.
WRITE 210-REPORT-REC FROM 690-BLANK-LINE
    AFTER ADVANCING 1 LINES.
```

Here we have again moved all of the report overhead to the bottom of the program. We did not have a first usage switch because the control report should only be executed once. We did not print the detail header line because it did not apply to the control information. We used the same page counter that we did on the detail lines because they come out on the same report file.

This is our basic program. It is our contention that this basic program can serve as a base line for any batch program that you will encounter. In the rest of this text, we will try to prove this theory.

Chapter 7

Modifying the Basic COBOL Program

As we stated in chapter one, a major characteristic of a good program is adaptability. It must be flexible and easy to modify. Adaptability is the prime consideration of the coding methods that we have used so far.

In a maintenance and enhancement environment, it is critical that a program be easy to read and understand. A maintenance programmer might work on a hundred different programs in a year. He might work on the same program every other week, and not see other programs for years. A simple change to a file layout can effect half of the programs in a 500 module system.

In the meantime, the backlog of work is growing, and growing, and growing. The users have become more sophisticated, especially after using spreadsheets and small databases with HTML, and want the mainframe system to do more. The rules of the business change, and so the system has to change. New systems are installed, meaning more new programs have to be supported.

And then an important transaction tape flips off the reel and wraps itself around the spindle. Ever see the results when a cassette tape wraps itself around the spindle. Imagine what 45 feet of crumpled computer tape looks like. It took a very long weekend to rebuild that file.

Bottom line, the programmer does not have time to spend two days trying to figure out what a program does before he can change it. To alleviate this problem we need to reduce the percentage of the program that the maintenance programmer has to understand to do his job.

By using coupling and cohesion we can develop Functionally Cohesive modules that are linked together by Sequentially Cohesive drive modules. These drive modules then serve as an outline of the program. This design also make adding or deleting functions as simple as plugging them in or taking them out. Let's examine the process of modifying our basic program by reviewing four different ways to fulfill a users request.

Our user wishes to have the employee's name on the report, along with the employee number which is already on the report. This is a reasonable request, but it is outside the requirements that we used to write the original program. The data is also not available on the input file. This will require us to obtain the employee's name from an outside source. Since this is a single function we will add a new cohesive paragraph to our program. We will label the new paragraph B300-GET-EMPLOYEE-NAME. Adding this new paragraph to the B000-MAIN-PROCESS will give us the following paragraph.

```
B000-MAIN-PROCESS.
PERFORM X100-READ-INPUT-RECORD
PERFORM UNTIL 310-END-OF-FILE-FLAG = 'Y'
     PERFORM B200-COMPUTE-COMMISSION
     PERFORM B400-LOAD-REPORT-LINE
     PERFORM Y100-WRITE-REPORT-LINE
     PERFORM B300-GET-EMPLOYEE-NAME
     PERFORM B500-LOAD-OUTPUT-RECORD
     PERFORM X200-WRITE-OUTPUT-RECORD
     PERFORM X100-READ-INPUT-RECORD
END-PERFORM.
```

We will also add a line to paragraph B400-LOAD-REPORT-LINE:

MOVE 410-EMPLOYEE-NAME TO 615-EMPLOYEE-NAME

where 410-EMPLOYEE-NAME is a working storage field that will hold the EMPLOYEE NAME between the end of the search and the time where we move it to the new report line field 615-EMPLOYEE-NAME.

Paragraph B300-GET-EMPLOYEE-NAME will be used to get the data that we want from the external source. What that source is, or how we access that source, does not effect the rest of the logic flow. We could use any access method, and the only areas that change are those parts of the program which define or manipulate the input source.

We will demonstrate this by using four different access methods. The first access method will be the use of a predefined internal table. The second method will be an internal program table that is loaded from an input file at the beginning of the program. The third method will be a call to a subroutine. The fourth method will be a call to an external database.

In the first method, using a predefined internal table, we begin by defining a table in working storage.

```
01  810-EMPLOYEE-NAME-TABLE-AREA.
    05  810-SUBSR                PIC 9(03) VALUE ZEROES.
    05  810-LOAD                 PIC 9(03) VALUE 4.
    05  810-LIMIT                PIC 9(03) VALUE 4.
    05  810-EMPLOYEE-TBL-DATA.
        07  FILLER PIC X(20) VALUE '11111 W.T. DOOR   '.
        07  FILLER PIC X(20) VALUE '22222 WILLIAM PENN'.
        07  FILLER PIC X(20) VALUE '33333 JANE DOE    '.
        07  FILLER PIC X(20) VALUE '44444 JOHN DOE    '.
    05  810-EMPLOYEE-TABLE
        810-EMPLOYEE-TBL-DATA.
        07  810-EMPLOYEE-TBL-ROW  OCCURS 4 TIMES
                                  INDEXED BY 810-INDEX.
            09  810-EMPLOYEE-NBR    PIC X(05).
            09  FILLER              PIC X(01).
            09  810-EMPLOYEE-NAME   PIC X(14).
```

Again we have linked all of the fields that are used to process this table together in a functionally cohesive module. The 810- prefix helps the programmer to know that any field that they encounter in the procedure division with that prefix belongs to this table. With the table defined, we can write the B300 paragraph to process the search.

```
***********************************************************************************
*** PROC GETS THE EMPLOYEE NAME FOR THE INPUT EMPLOYEE NBR***
*** FROM THE HARD CODED EMPLOYEE NAME TABLE.              ***
***********************************************************************************
B300-GET-EMPLOYEE-NAME.
     MOVE 'NAME NOT FOUND' TO 410-EMPLOYEE-NAME.
     PERFORM VARYING 810-SUB FROM 1 BY 1
               UNTIL 810-SUB GREATER THAN 810-LOAD
               OR 410-EMPLOYEE-NAME
                    NOT EQUAL 'NAME NOT FOUND'
          IF 810-EMPLOYEE-NBR(810-SUB) = 910-EMPLOYEE-NBR
          MOVE 810-EMPLOYEE-NAME(810-SUB)
               TO 410-EMPLOYEE-NAME
          END-IF
     END-PERFORM.
```

We could have used the COBOL "SEARCH" verb, but we built this perform so that we could show the process. We also wanted to point out that by initializing the field we are trying to populate we can use it as a control field rather than defining a separate flag. Otherwise the paragraph would have looked like this:

```
B300-GET-EMPLOYEE-NAME.
     MOVE 'N'                    TO 310-EMPLOYEE-FOUND-FLAG
     PERFORM VARYING 810-SUB FROM 1 BY 1
               UNTIL 810-SUB GREATER THAN 810-LOAD
               OR 310-EMPLOYEE-FOUND-FLAG = 'Y'
          IF 810-EMPLOYEE-NBR(810-SUB) = 910-EMPLOYEE-NBR
          MOVE 810-EMPLOYEE-NAME(810-SUB)
               TO 410-EMPLOYEE-NAME
          MOVE 'Y' TO 310-EMPLOYEE-FOUND-FLAG
```

```
      END-IF
   END-PERFORM.
   IF 310-EMPLOYEE-FOUND-FLAG = 'N'
      MOVE 'NAME NOT FOUND'  TO 410-EMPLOYEE-NAME
   END-IF.
```

This method forces us to use an artificial control field which is both redundant and external to our field definition area.

We should also note how our prefixes allowed us to use the extended field name (EMPLOYEE-NAME and EMPLOYEE-NBR) for the same data value while allowing the different working storage addresses to be unique:

   410- program specific working storage field
   615- employee fields on the report detail line
   810- employee table
   910- main input file
   930- employee input file.

In the second method we will change the program to use a table built from an external file. This requires that we change the program by removing the hard coded values from the working storage table and adding the code to do the initial load of the table. The table is changed to look like this.

```
01 810-EMPLOYEE-NAME-TABLE-AREA.
    05 810-SUBSR          PIC 9(03) VALUE ZEROES.
    05 810-LOAD           PIC 9(03) VALUE ZEROES.
    05 810-LIMIT          PIC 9(03) VALUE 100.
    05 810-EMPLOYEE-TABLE.
        07 810-EMPLOYEE-TBL-ROW  OCCURS 100 TIMES
                                 INDEXED BY 810-INDEX.
            09 810-EMPLOYEE-NBR      PIC X(05).
            09 FILLER                PIC X(01).
            09 810-EMPLOYEE-NAME     PIC X(14).
```

We have removed the predefined table values, and changed the initial value of 810-LOAD from 4 to 0, since the table is not loaded yet. We then add the FD,

```
FD  110-EMPLOYEE-TABLE-FILE
    BLOCK CONTAINS 0 RECORDS
    RECORDING MODE IS F
    RECORD CONTAINS 80 CHARACTERS
    LABEL RECORDS ARE STANDARD.
01  110-EMPLOYEE-TABLE-REC  PIC X(80).
```

the input file work area,

```
01  930-EMPLOYEE-INPUT-AREA.
    05  930-EMPLOYEE-NBR     PIC X(05).
    05  930-EMPLOYEE-NAME    PIC X(14).
```

and the utility paragraph to read the input file.

```
X300-READ-EMPLOYEE-FILE.
    READ 110-EMPLOYEE-TABLE-FILE INTO 930-EMPLOYEE-INPUT-AREA
        AT END MOVE 'Y' TO 310-END-OF-EMPLOYEE-FILE.
```

We can then build the process to load the table from the input file. Again, this is a single process, so we will build a single functionally cohesive module. We will also label it as an initialization paragraph.

```
**************************************************************************
*** PROC LOADS THE EMPLOYEE NAME AND NUMBER TABLE FROM    ***
*** THE INPUT FILE                                        ***
**************************************************************************
A200-LOAD-EMPLOYEE-TABLE.
    OPEN INPUT 110-EMPLOYEE-TABLE-FILE.
    MOVE 'N' TO 310-END-OF-EMPLOYEE-FILE
    MOVE 0 TO 810-LOAD
    PERFORM X300-READ-EMPLOYEE-FILE.
    PERFORM UNTIL 310-END-OF-EMPLOYEE-FILE = 'Y'
```

```
      PERFORM A210-LOAD-EMPLOYEE-ROW
      PERFORM X300-READ-EMPLOYEE-FILE
   END-PERFORM.
   CLOSE    110-EMPLOYEE-TABLE-FILE.

A210-LOAD-EMPLOYEE-ROW.
   IF 810-LOAD LESS THAN 800-LIMIT
      ADD 1 TO 800-LOAD
      MOVE 930-EMPLOYEE-NBR  TO 810-EMPLOYEE-NBR (810-LOAD)
      MOVE 930-EMPLOYEE-NAME TO 810-EMPLOYEE-NAME(810-LOAD)
   ELSE
      PERFORM Z100-TABLE-OVERFLOW-ABEND
   END-IF.
```

Here we again initialize our loop by reading the first employee record, and use it to load the first row. We then check to make sure that we will not exceed the length of our table before we increment the 800-LOAD counter. This allows us to avoid loading data past the end of the defined table area.

If the table overflow condition is encountered, we will execute the assigned abend paragraph. This paragraph will display the appropriate diagnostic messages and cause the program to abend. (The messages will be very important to the unfortunate programmer who is on call when the table overflows. Causing someone to have to debug a table overflow without proper displays at 2 in the morning is not a good way to make friends among your co-workers.)

While this Z200 paragraph is a required piece of code, it should not be executed during the normal course of processing (In fact, it should never be executed). This is why we placed it at the end of the house keeping functions.

B300-GET-EMPLOYEE-NAME is not changed from the previous example. The program will use the 800-LOAD field as one of its processing limits, since it represents the number of data rows that were actually loaded. Changing the source of the table data does not effect any other processing. While they deal with the same data, they are independent processes, and are placed in independent modules.

If a number of different programs need to read the employee name from a table that is loaded from this file, we can save a great deal of coding time and effort by placing the table search into an independent subprogram.

The procedure division of this subroutine would look like this:

```
PROCEDURE DIVISION USING 910-EMPLOYEE-NBR
                          910-EMPLOYEE-NAME.
     IF 810-TABLE-LOAD = 0
        PERFORM A200-LOAD-EMPLOYEE-TABLE.
     END-IF.
     PERFORM B300-GET-EMPLOYEE-NAME.
     GOBACK.


*******************************************************************************
*** PROC LOADS THE EMPLOYEE NAME AND NUMBER TABLE FROM   ***
*** THE INPUT FILE                                        ***
*******************************************************************************
A200-LOAD-EMPLOYEE-TABLE.
     OPEN INPUT 110-EMPLOYEE-TABLE-FILE.
     MOVE 'N' TO 310-END-OF-EMPLOYEE-FILE
     PERFORM X300-READ-EMPLOYEE-FILE.
     PERFORM UNTIL 310-END-OF-EMPLOYEE-FILE = 'Y'
        PERFORM A210-LOAD-EMPLOYEE-ROW
        PERFORM X300-READ-EMPLOYEE-FILE
     END-PERFORM.
     CLOSE         110-EMPLOYEE-TABLE-FILE.

A210-LOAD-EMPLOYEE-ROW.
     IF 810-LOAD LESS THAN 800-LIMIT
        ADD 1 TO 800-LOAD
        MOVE 930-EMPLOYEE-NBR  TO 810-EMPLOYEE-NBR (810-LOAD)
        MOVE 930-EMPLOYEE-NAME TO 810-EMPLOYEE-NAME(810-LOAD)
     END-IF.
```

```
***********************************************************************************************
*** PROC GETS THE EMPLOYEE NAME FOR THE INPUT EMPLOYEE    ***
*** NUMBER FROM THE INTERNAL TABLE THAT WAS LOADED EARLIER***
***********************************************************************************************
B300-GET-EMPLOYEE-NAME.
        MOVE 'NAME NOT FOUND' TO 910-EMPLOYEE-NAME.
        PERFORM VARYING 810-SUB FROM 1 BY 1
                UNTIL 810-SUB GREATER THAN 810-LOAD
                OR 910-EMPLOYEE-NAME
                    NOT EQUAL 'NAME NOT FOUND'
                IF 810-EMPLOYEE-NBR(810-SUB) = 910-EMPLOYEE-NBR
                    MOVE 810-EMPLOYEE-NAME(810-SUB)
                        TO 910-EMPLOYEE-NAME
                END-IF
        END-PERFORM.
```

The working storage of a linked subroutine will remain unchanged during processing of the main stream job. This allows us to load the table from the external source on the first call. We will then use this table on each subsequent call. The B300-GET-EMPLOYEE-NAME in our main program will be reduced to.

```
B300-GET-EMPLOYEE-NAME.
        CALL 'EMPNAME' USING 910-EMPLOYEE-NBR
                             410-EMPLOYEE-NAME.
```

Again, only this portion of the program is effected. The B400- paragraph will still use the 410-EMPLOYEE-NAME to populate the output file.

In our fourth example will be a call to an employee database to get the employee name.

```
B300-GET-EMPLOYEE-NAME.
        MOVE 910-EMPLOYEE-NBR    TO 510-EMPLOYEE-NBR
        SELECT  EMPLOYEE_NAME
          INTO :410-EMPLOYEE-NAME
          FROM  VHA_EMPLOYEE_NAME
         WHERE  EMPLOYEE-NBR     = 510-EMPLOYEE-NBR
```

```
IF SQL-CODE = 0
   NEXT SENTENCE
ELSE
   IF SQL-CODE = 100
      MOVE 'NAME NOT DEFINED' TO 410-EMPLOYEE-NAME
   ELSE
      MOVE 'SQL ERROR ON EMPLOYEE READ' TO ABEND-MSG
      PERFORM Z999-ABEND
END-IF.
```

As you can see, this paragraph can be split into two separate functions. We have a data manipulation portion which sets the database request key and checks the return code to set the value. We also have a house keeping function which handles the call to the database access program, checks the return code for an abnormal return, and if necessary, abends the program. Moving the housekeeping functions to a WXXX- series paragraph gives us the following listing.

```
B300-GET-EMPLOYEE-NAME.
   MOVE 910-EMPLOYEE-NBR    TO 510-EMPLOYEE-NBR
   PERFORM W110-READ-EMPLOYEE-FILE.
   IF SQL-CODE = 100
      MOVE 'NAME NOT DEFINED' TO 410-EMPLOYEE-NAME
   END-IF.

W110-READ-EMPLOYEE-FILE.
   SELECT  EMPLOYEE_NAME
      INTO :410-EMPLOYEE-NAME
      FROM  VHA_EMPLOYEE_NAME
      WHERE  EMPLOYEE-NBR     = 510-EMPLOYEE-NBR

   IF SQL-CODE = 000
   OR SQL-CODE = 100
      NEXT SENTENCE
   ELSE
      MOVE 'SQL ERROR ON EMPLOYEE READ' TO ABEND-MSG
      PERFORM Z999-ABEND
   END-IF.
```

Since these housekeeping functions are common whenever we access this database, we can build the access routines and save them as separate modules. These separate modules are called "copylibs" or "includes" depending on the program editor that is being used.

We can then bring these predefined and tested modules into our program whenever we need them. Doing this saves us the time needed to code and test the required routines. This in turn reduces the cost of program development and maintenance.

From these examples we see the benefits of building programs as a combination of functionally cohesive execution modules linked together in sequentially cohesive drive modules. Even though we changed the source of the employee name field four times, none of the rest of the program was effected. This saved us the effort of having to understand the rest of the program. This also eliminated the need for regression testing to find out what we broke along the way.

In the next chapter we will use this technique to add more functions to our basic program.

Chapter 8

Adding Functions to the Basic COBOL Program

As we stated before, the basic program can serve as a skeleton for any application. In this chapter we will show this by adding more functions to the program. For example, the user now wishes to produce a management level report along with the detail report. This report will show only those items whose unit price is over $100.00. We will continue to produce the detail report for each input record. We will add the appropriate FD, and the working storage for the new report definition.

```
FD  230-REPORT-FILE
    BLOCK CONTAINS 0 RECORDS
    RECORD CONTAINS 133 CHARACTERS
    RECORDING MODE IS F
    LABEL RECORDS ARE STANDARD
    DATA RECORD IS 230-REPORT-RECORD.
01  230-REPORT-RECORD    PIC X(133).
```

```
********************************************************************************
*** THIS AREA IS USED TO DEFINE THE MANAGEMENT COMMISSION RPT ***
********************************************************************************
```

```
01  630-MGT-COMMISSION-REPORT.
    05  630-FIRST-USAGE        PIC X(01)           VALUE 'Y'.
    05  630-LINE-COUNT         PIC 9(02) COMP-3 VALUE 77.
```

```
05 630-LINE-LIMIT           PIC 9(02) COMP-3 VALUE 60.
05 630-PAGE-COUNTER         PIC 9(05) COMP-3 VALUE ZEROES.
05 631-HEADER-LINE.
   07 FILLER                PIC X(01) VALUE SPACES.
   07 FILLER                PIC X(08) VALUE 'PROGRAM1'.
   07 FILLER                PIC X(25) VALUE SPACES.
   07 631-HEADER-LITERAL    PIC X(30) VALUE SPACES.
   07 FILLER                PIC X(15) VALUE SPACES.
   07 631-CURRENT-DATE.
      09 631-CURRENT-MM     PIC X(02) VALUE SPACES.
      09 FILLER             PIC X(01) VALUE '/'.
      09 631-CURRENT-DD     PIC X(02) VALUE SPACES.
      09 FILLER             PIC X(01) VALUE '/'.
      09 631-CURRENT-YY     PIC X(02) VALUE SPACES.
   07 FILLER                PIC X(03) VALUE SPACES.
   07 FILLER                PIC X(05) VALUE 'PAGE'.
   07 631-PAGE-NUMBER       PIC ZZZZ9 VALUE ZEROES.


05 634-DETAIL-HEADER.
   07 FILLER    PIC X(05)   VALUE SPACES.
   07 FILLER    PIC X(05)   VALUE 'EMPNO'.
   07 FILLER    PIC X(01)   VALUE SPACES.
   07 FILLER    PIC X(20)   VALUE 'EMPLOYEE NAME'.
   07 FILLER    PIC X(02)   VALUE SPACES.
   07 FILLER    PIC X(07)   VALUE 'CATALOG'.
   07 FILLER    PIC X(02)   VALUE SPACES.
   07 FILLER    PIC X(07)   VALUE ' PRICE'.
   07 FILLER    PIC X(02)   VALUE SPACES.
   07 FILLER    PIC X(05)   VALUE 'QUANT'.
   07 FILLER    PIC X(02)   VALUE SPACES.
   07 FILLER    PIC X(08)   VALUE 'TOT SALE'.
   07 FILLER    PIC X(02)   VALUE SPACES.
   07 FILLER    PIC X(08)   VALUE 'COMM AMT'.


05 635-DETAIL-LINE.
   07 FILLER                PIC X(05)   VALUE SPACES.
   07 635-EMPLOYEE-NBR      PIC X(05)   VALUE SPACES.
   07 FILLER                PIC X(01)   VALUE SPACES.
   07 635-EMPLOYEE-NAME     PIC X(20)   VALUE SPACES.
   07 FILLER                PIC X(02)   VALUE SPACES.
```

```
07 635-CATALOG-NBR       PIC X(06)      VALUE SPACES.
07 FILLER                PIC X(02)      VALUE SPACES.
07 635-UNIT-PRICE        PIC ZZZ9V99    VALUE ZEROES.
07 FILLER                PIC X(02)      VALUE SPACES.
07 635-NUMBER-SOLD       PIC ZZZZ9      VALUE ZEROES.
07 FILLER                PIC X(02)      VALUE SPACES.
07 635-SALES-AMT         PIC ZZZZ9V99   VALUE ZEROES.
07 FILLER                PIC X(02)      VALUE SPACES.
07 635-COMMISSION-AMT    PIC ZZZZ9V99   VALUE ZEROES.
```

We should note that this report definition is functionally cohesive in that it is completely self contained. All of the fields needed to produce this report are contained within the structure.

The paragraph that handles the writing of the report line (Y400-WRITE-MANAGEMENT-RPT) will also be a clone of the report writing paragraph in the basic program (Y100-WRITE-REPORT-LINE) which we can simply rename to Y100-WRITE-DETAIL-RPT. This will make it easier to differentiate between the two reports. We will also write the following simple paragraph to load the new report line.

```
B600-LOAD-MANAGEMENT-REPORT.
    MOVE 910-EMPLOYEE-NBR    TO  635-EMPLOYEE-NBR.
    MOVE 410-EMPLOYEE-NAME   TO  635-EMPLOYEE-NAME.
    MOVE 910-UNIT-PRICE      TO  635-UNIT-PRICE.
    MOVE 910-CATALOG-NBR     TO  635-CATALOG-NBR.
    MOVE 910-NUMBER-SOLD     TO  635-NUMBER-SOLD.
    MOVE 410-SALES-AMT       TO  635-SALES-AMT.
    MOVE 410-COMMISSION-AMT  TO  635-COMMISSION-AMT.
```

The same input fields were used to populate as both the original report line and the new report line. While the process to populate both report lines is similar, they are still independent of each other. The elimination of the field "635-SALES-AMT" on the management report will not affect the processing of the detail report. The addition of this process will cause our main drive paragraph to expand as follows.

```
B000-MAIN-PROCESS.
    PERFORM X100-READ-INPUT-RECORD
    PERFORM UNTIL 310-END-OF-FILE-FLAG = 'Y'
        PERFORM B200-COMPUTE-COMMISSION
        PERFORM B300-GET-EMPLOYEE-NAME
        PERFORM B400-LOAD-REPORT-LINE
        PERFORM B500-LOAD-OUTPUT-RECORD
        PERFORM Y100-WRITE-DETAIL-RPT
        PERFORM Y200-WRITE-OUTPUT-RECORD
        IF 910-UNIT-PRICE >= 100.00
            PERFORM B600-LOAD-MANAGEMENT-REPORT
            PERFORM Y400-WRITE-MANAGEMENT-RPT
        END-IF
        PERFORM X100-READ-INPUT-RECORD
    END-PERFORM.
```

Or if we wish to simplify the main paragraph we could move the IF statement to the B600- paragraph.

```
B000-MAIN-PROCESS.
    PERFORM X100-READ-INPUT-RECORD
    PERFORM UNTIL 310-END-OF-FILE-FLAG = 'Y'
        PERFORM B200-COMPUTE-COMMISSION
        PERFORM B300-GET-EMPLOYEE-NAME
        PERFORM B400-LOAD-REPORT-LINE
        PERFORM B500-LOAD-OUTPUT-RECORD
        PERFORM Y100-WRITE-DETAIL-RPT
        PERFORM Y200-WRITE-OUTPUT-RECORD
        PERFORM B600-BUILD-MANAGEMENT-REPORT
        PERFORM X100-READ-INPUT-RECORD
    END-PERFORM.

B600-BUILD-MANAGEMENT-REPORT.
    IF 910-UNIT-PRICE >= 100.00
        PERFORM B610-LOAD-MANAGEMENT-RPT-LINE
        PERFORM Y400-WRITE-MANAGEMENT-RPT
    END-IF.
```

```
B610-LOAD-MANAGEMENT-RPT-LINE.
    MOVE 910-EMPLOYEE-NBR     TO 635-EMPLOYEE-NBR.
    MOVE 410-EMPLOYEE-NAME  TO 635-EMPLOYEE-NAME.
    MOVE 910-UNIT-PRICE       TO 635-UNIT-PRICE.
    MOVE 910-CATALOG-NBR      TO 635-CATALOG-NBR.
    MOVE 910-NUMBER-SOLD      TO 635-NUMBER-SOLD.
    MOVE 410-SALES-AMT        TO 635-SALES-AMT.
    MOVE 410-COMMISSION-AMT TO 635-COMMISSION-AMT.
```

But this being a management report, the user only wants to see the employee name and number once per block. For this example, we will assume that the records will come into the program in employee number order, and we will change the report layout as follows:

```
*****************************************************************************************
*** THIS AREA IS USED TO DEFINE THE MANAGEMENT COMMISSION RPT   ***
*****************************************************************************************
01  630-MGT-SALES-REPORT.
    05  630-FIRST-USAGE           PIC X(01)          VALUE 'Y'.
    05  630-LINE-COUNT            PIC 9(02) COMP-3 VALUE 77.
    05  630-LINE-LIMIT            PIC 9(02) COMP-3 VALUE 60.
    05  630-PAGE-COUNTER          PIC 9(05) COMP-3 VALUE ZEROES.
    05  630-PREV-EMPLOYEE-NBR  PIC X(05)  VALUE SPACES.
    05  631-HEADER-LINE.
        07  FILLER                PIC X(01) VALUE SPACES.
        07  FILLER                PIC X(08) VALUE 'PROGRAM1'.
        07  FILLER                PIC X(25) VALUE SPACES.
        07  631-HEADER-LITERAL PIC X(30) VALUE SPACES.
        07  FILLER                PIC X(15) VALUE SPACES.
        07  631-CURRENT-DATE.
            09  631-CURRENT-MM PIC X(02)  VALUE SPACES.
            09  FILLER            PIC X(01) VALUE '/'.
            09  631-CURRENT-DD PIC X(02)  VALUE SPACES.
            09  FILLER            PIC X(01) VALUE '/'.
            09  631-CURRENT-YY PIC X(02)  VALUE SPACES.
        07  FILLER                PIC X(03) VALUE SPACES.
        07  FILLER                PIC X(05) VALUE 'PAGE'.
        07  631-PAGE-NUMBER    PIC ZZZZ9 VALUE ZEROES.
```

```
05  633-DETAIL-HEADER.
    07  FILLER    PIC X(05)  VALUE SPACES.
    07  FILLER    PIC X(07)  VALUE 'CATALOG'.
    07  FILLER    PIC X(02)  VALUE SPACES.
    07  FILLER    PIC X(07)  VALUE ' PRICE'.
    07  FILLER    PIC X(02)  VALUE SPACES.
    07  FILLER    PIC X(05)  VALUE 'QUANT'.
    07  FILLER    PIC X(02)  VALUE SPACES.
    07  FILLER    PIC X(08)  VALUE 'TOT SALE'.
    07  FILLER    PIC X(02)  VALUE SPACES.
    07  FILLER    PIC X(08)  VALUE 'COMM AMT'.

05  634-EMPLOYEE-LINE.
    07  FILLER                PIC X(05)     VALUE SPACES.
    07  FILLER                PIC X(08)     VALUE 'EMPLOYEE'.
    07  634-EMPLOYEE-NBR      PIC X(05)     VALUE SPACES.
    07  FILLER                PIC X(01)     VALUE SPACES.
    07  634-EMPLOYEE-NAME     PIC X(20)     VALUE SPACES.

05  635-DETAIL-LINE.
    07  FILLER                PIC X(05)     VALUE SPACES.
    07  635-CATALOG-NBR       PIC X(06)     VALUE SPACES.
    07  FILLER                PIC X(02)     VALUE SPACES.
    07  635-UNIT-PRICE        PIC ZZZ9V99   VALUE ZEROES.
    07  FILLER                PIC X(02)     VALUE SPACES.
    07  635-NUMBER-SOLD       PIC ZZZZ9     VALUE ZEROES.
    07  FILLER                PIC X(02)     VALUE SPACES.
    07  635-SALES-AMT         PIC ZZZZ9V99  VALUE ZEROES.
    07  FILLER                PIC X(02)     VALUE SPACES.
    07  635-COMMISSION-AMT    PIC ZZZZ9V99  VALUE ZEROES.
```

The production of the employee header record is independent of the loading of the report data. But it is involved in the production of the report lines and header. Since this is a header process, we will not change the main line paragraph B600-BUILD-MANAGEMENT-REPORT (except to make the required changes to the prefix of some of the data names). We will make the change in the report writer paragraph.

```
*******************************************************************************
*** PARAGRAPH WRITES OUT THE DETAIL LINE TO THE REPORT      ***
*** AFTER IT CHECKS THE LINE COUNT AGAINST THE LINE SIZE    ***
*******************************************************************************
Y400-WRITE-MANAGEMENT-REPORT.
    ADD 1 TO 630-LINE-COUNTER.
    IF 630-LINE-COUNTER GREATER THAN 630-LINE-LIMIT
        PERFORM Y410-WRITE-PAGE-HEADER
        PERFORM Y420-WRITE-EMPLOYEE-LN
    ELSE
        IF 910-EMPLOYEE-NBR NOT EQUAL 630-PREV-EMPLOYEE-NBR
            IF 630-LINE-COUNTER > (630-LINE-LIMIT—2)
                WRITE 210-REPORT-REC FROM  690-BLANK-LINE
                    AFTER ADVANCING 1 LINES
                ADD 1 TO 630-LINE-COUNTER
                PERFORM Y420-WRITE-EMPLOYEE-LN
        ELSE
                PERFORM Y410-WRITE-PAGE-HEADER
                PERFORM Y420-WRITE-EMPLOYEE-LN
        END-IF
        END-IF
    END-IF.

    WRITE 210-REPORT-REC FROM 615-DETAIL-LINE
        AFTER ADVANCING 1 LINES.

Y420-WRITE-EMPLOYEE-LN.
    MOVE  910-EMPLOYEE-NBR TO 630-PREV-EMPLOYEE-NBR
    WRITE 210-REPORT-REC FROM  634-EMPLOYEE-LINE
        AFTER ADVANCING 1 LINES.
    ADD 1 TO 630-LINE-COUNTER.
```

The program will write the employee line on the first page, with each subsequent page break, and when the input employee number changes. The program will also check its position on the page before it writes the report line to make sure that it does not write an employee line as the last line of the page. We included the employee line logic in the report writer logic because it is independent of the loading of the report line, but it is dependent on the timing of the writing of the report header and the report detail line. We can also simplify these paragraphs as follows:

```
*********************************************************************************
*** PARAGRAPH WRITES OUT THE DETAIL LINE TO THE REPORT      ***
*** AFTER IT CHECKS THE LINE COUNT AGAINST THE LINE SIZE     ***
*********************************************************************************
Y400-WRITE-MANAGEMENT-REPORT.
     PERFORM Y410-CHECK-BREAKS
     IF 630-PAGE-BREAK    = 'Y'
         PERFORM Y420-WRITE-PAGE-HEADER.
     IF 630-EMPLOYEE-BREAK = 'Y'
         PERFORM Y430-WRITE-EMPLOYEE-LN.

     WRITE 210-REPORT-REC FROM 635-DETAIL-LINE
         AFTER ADVANCING 1 LINES.


Y410-CHECK-BREAKS
     ADD    1 TO 630-LINE-COUNTER.
     MOVE 'N' TO 630-PAGE-BREAK
     MOVE 'N' TO 630-EMPLOYEE-BREAK

     IF 910-EMPLOYEE-NBR NOT EQUAL 630-PREV-EMPLOYEE-NBR
         MOVE 'Y' TO 630-EMPLOYEE-BREAK
         IF 630-LINE-COUNTER > (630-LINE-LIMIT—2)
             MOVE 'Y' TO 630-PAGE-BREAK.

     IF 630-LINE-COUNTER GREATER THAN 630-LINE-LIMIT
         MOVE 'Y' TO 630-PAGE-BREAK
         MOVE 'Y' TO 630-EMPLOYEE-BREAK.

Y430-WRITE-EMPLOYEE-LN.
     MOVE 910-EMPLOYEE-NBR TO 630-PREV-EMPLOYEE-NBR
     IF 630-PAGE-BREAK = 'N'
         WRITE 230-REPORT-REC FROM 690-BLANK-LINE
             AFTER ADVANCING 1 LINES.
```

```
WRITE 230-REPORT-REC FROM  634-EMPLOYEE-LINE
      AFTER ADVANCING 1 LINES.
ADD 1 TO 630-LINE-COUNTER.
```

Here we see a good use of control coupling. In the Y410- paragraph, we determine which (if any) of the report breaks need to be taken. Inside the paragraph it doesn't matter if we find one or two conditions which will fulfill the employee line break request. Either or both of the conditions will set the flag to "Y", which in turn will trigger the writing of the employee header line. The page break flag will also tell the program if it needs a blank line before the employee line. This blank line separates the employee line from the last block of employee data. It is not needed after a page break because the page break writes its own blank line.

This level of coupling is acceptable because it is occurring between two functionally cohesive modules, which are in turn is part of a larger functional cohesive module (Y400-WRITE-MANAGEMENT-REPORT). The two flags do not affect processing outside of this area.

We could also add logic to write our report to a flat file as a backup, as well as writing it to the print queue. Again we will do this in the print routine, because the function is dependent on the print lines, and not on the processing of the rest of the program.

```
*****************************************************************************
*** PARAGRAPH WRITES OUT THE DETAIL LINE TO THE REPORT    ***
*** AFTER IT CHECKS THE LINE COUNT AGAINST THE LINE SIZE  ***
*****************************************************************************
Y400-WRITE-MANAGEMENT-REPORT.
    PERFORM Y410-CHECK-BREAKS
    IF 630-PAGE-BREAK    = 'Y'
       PERFORM Y420-WRITE-PAGE-HEADER.
    IF 630-EMPLOYEE-BREAK = 'Y'
       PERFORM Y430-WRITE-EMPLOYEE-LN.

    MOVE 635-DETAIL-LINE TO 630-OUTPUT-LINE
    PERFORM Y490-PHYSICAL-OUTPUT.
```

```
Y410-CHECK-BREAKS
    MOVE 'N' TO 630-PAGE-BREAK
    MOVE 'N' TO 630-EMPLOYEE-BREAK

    IF 910-EMPLOYEE-NBR NOT EQUAL 630-PREV-EMPLOYEE-NBR
        MOVE 'Y' TO 630-EMPLOYEE-BREAK
        IF 630-LINE-COUNTER > (630-LINE-LIMIT—2)
            MOVE 'Y' TO 630-PAGE-BREAK.

    IF 630-LINE-COUNTER GREATER THAN 630-LINE-LIMIT
        MOVE 'Y' TO 630-PAGE-BREAK
        MOVE 'Y' TO 630-EMPLOYEE-BREAK.

Y430-WRITE-EMPLOYEE-LN.
    MOVE 910-EMPLOYEE-NBR TO 630-PREV-EMPLOYEE-NBR
    IF 630-PAGE-BREAK = 'N'
        MOVE 690-BLANK-LINE TO 630-OUTPUT-LINE
        PERFORM Y490-PHYSICAL-OUTPUT.

    MOVE 634-EMPLOYEE-LINE TO 630-OUTPUT-LINE
    PERFORM Y490-PHYSICAL-OUTPUT.

Y490-PHYSICAL-OUTPUT.
    WRITE 230-REPORT-REC FROM 630-OUTPUT-LINE
            AFTER ADVANCING 1 LINES.
    ADD 1 TO 630-LINE-COUNTER.
    WRITE 250-BACKUP-REC FROM 630-OUTPUT-LINE.
```

Here the physical output paragraph handles the overhead of writing both copies of the output line to the two different output areas. We have also moved the code to increment the line counter to this paragraph to centralize the function. This helps to make the program easier to read.

But what is the benefit of having a management report if you can't see how your group is doing as compared to the other groups? So we will add a function to check the division of each employee, and sort the input records by division and employee. We will begin by adding the sort definition code to the data definition:

```
SD  130-SORT-FILE.

01  130-SORT-RECORD.
    05  130-EMPLOYEE-DIVISION   PIC 9(03).
    05  130-EMPLOYEE-NUMBER     PIC X(05).
    05  130-CATALOG-NUMBER      PIC X(06).
    05  130-UNIT-PRICE          PIC 9(04)V99.
    05  130-NUMBER-SOLD         PIC 9(05).
    05  130-TOTAL-SALES         PIC 9(05)V99.
```

This change will only affect the main drive paragraph. This is because each module is independent of the other modules.

```
A000-MAIN-PROCESS.
    SORT SORT-RECORD BY  130-EMPLOYEE-DIVISION
                         130-EMPLOYEE-NBR
        INPUT PROCEDURE B000-INPUT-PROCEDURE
                        C000-OUTPUT-PROCEDURE.


**************************************************************************************
*** AREA BUILDS AND RELEASES THE SORT RECORD.                                ***
**************************************************************************************
B000-INPUT-PROCEDURE.
    PERFORM X100-READ-INPUT-RECORD
    PERFORM UNTIL 310-END-OF-FILE-FLAG = 'Y'
        PERFORM B100-INIT-SORT-RECORD
        PERFORM B200-GET-DIVISION
        PERFORM X200-RELEASE-SORT-RECORD
        PERFORM X100-READ-INPUT-RECORD
    END-PERFORM.


***========================================================***
*** PROC LOADS THE SORT RECORD WITH DATA FROM THE INPUT ***
*** PROC ALSO INITIALIZES THE DIVISION FIELD.          ***
***========================================================***
B100-INIT-SORT-RECORD.
    MOVE ZEROES                    TO 130-EMPLOYEE-DIVISION
```

```
        MOVE 910-EMPLOYEE-NUMBER TO 130-EMPLOYEE-NUMBER
        MOVE 910-CATALOG-NUMBER  TO 130-CATALOG-NUMBER
        MOVE 910-UNIT-PRICE      TO 130-UNIT-PRICE
        MOVE 910-NUMBER-SOLD     TO 130-NUMBER-SOLD
        MOVE 910-TOTAL-SALES     TO 130-TOTAL-SALES.


***======================================================***
*** PROC GETS THE DIVISION BY READING THE EMPLOYEE-DIVISION***
*** MASTER FILE.                                         ***
***======================================================***
 B200-GET-DIVISION.
        MOVE 910-EMPLOYEE-NBR TO 420-EMPLOYEE-NBR
        PERFORM W100-GET-EMPLOYEE-DIVISION.
        EVALUATE TRUE
            WHEN SQL-CODE = +000
                MOVE EMP-DIVISION TO 130-EMP-DIVISION
            WHEN SQL-CODE = +100
                MOVE 999          TO 130-EMP-DIVISION
        END-EVALUATE.


*************************************************************
*** AREA RETURNS THE SORT RECORD AND BUILDS THE REQUIRED ***
*** REPORTS.                                             ***
*************************************************************
 C000-OUTPUT-PROCEDURE.
        MOVE 'N' TO 310-END-OF-FILE-FLAG.
        PERFORM X500-RETURN-SORT-RECORD
        PERFORM UNTIL 310-END-OF-FILE-FLAG = 'Y'
            PERFORM C200-COMPUTE-COMMISSION
            PERFORM C300-GET-EMPLOYEE-NAME
            PERFORM C400-LOAD-REPORT-LINE
            PERFORM C500-LOAD-OUTPUT-RECORD
            PERFORM Y100-WRITE-DETAIL-RPT
            PERFORM Y200-WRITE-OUTPUT-RECORD
            PERFORM C600-LOAD-MANAGEMENT-REPORT
            PERFORM X500-RETURN-SORT-RECORD
        END-PERFORM.
```

```
***========================================================***
*** PROC HANDLES THE PHYSICAL RELEASE OF THE SORT RECORD ***
***========================================================***
X200-RELEASE-SORT-RECORD.
     RELEASE 130-SORT-RECORD.
     ADD 1 TO 300-SORT-RECORDS-RELEASED.


***========================================================***
*** PROC HANDLES THE PHYSICAL RETURN OF THE SORT RECORD ***
***========================================================***
X500-RETURN-SORT-RECORD.
     RETURN 130-SORT-RECORD.
     ADD 1 TO 300-SORT-RECORDS-RETURNED.
```

While we have made major changes to the design of the program, we have not made major changes to the underlying modules. This is true because each module is independent. The biggest change to the paragraphs in the report building process is to change the prefix numbers of the input fields so that the data comes from the sort file instead of from the input file.

We could also change the source of the input data to the sort routine, without making changes to the main program. Each of the read paragraphs are of course functionally cohesive modules that we store at the end of the program.

The changes to make this a VSAM program would all be contained in the X100-READ-INPUT paragraph.

The version of the program that uses CA/DATACOM tables would look like this:

```
*******************************************************************
*** AREA BUILDS AND RELEASES THE SORT RECORD FROM THE        ***
*** CA/DATACOM INPUT TABLES                                  ***
*******************************************************************
B000-INPUT-PROCEDURE.
     PERFORM W210-LOCATE-SALES-RECORD
```

```
PERFORM W220-OBTAIN-FIRST-SALES-RCD
PERFORM UNTIL 310-END-OF-FILE-FLAG = 'Y'
    PERFORM B100-INIT-SORT-RECORD
    PERFORM B200-GET-DIVISION
    PERFORM X200-RELEASE-SORT-RECORD
    PERFORM W230-OBTAIN-NEXT-SALES-RCD
END-PERFORM.
```

The new control paragraphs do the following. The W210 paragraph establishes position at the top of the table. The W220 paragraph reads the first record into the program, and checks for end of file. The W230 paragraph reads the next sequential record into the program, and checks for end of file.

The version of the program that uses DB2 tables would look like this:

```
****************************************************************************
*** AREA BUILDS AND RELEASES THE SORT RECORD FROM THE        ***
*** DB2 INPUT TABLES                                         ***
****************************************************************************
B000-INPUT-PROCEDURE.
    PERFORM W210-OPEN-CURSOR
    PERFORM W220-FETCH-CURSOR
    PERFORM UNTIL 310-END-OF-FILE-FLAG = 'Y'
        PERFORM B100-INIT-SORT-RECORD
        PERFORM B200-GET-DIVISION
        PERFORM X200-RELEASE-SORT-RECORD
        PERFORM W220-FETCH-CURSOR
    END-PERFORM.
```

The new control paragraphs do the following. The W210 paragraph establishes position at the top of the table. The W220 paragraph reads the record into the program, and checks for end of file.

By modularizing the individual program functions, we can minimize the number of changes that have to be made to change a program's total functionality. In the next chapter we will use our modular programming techniques on the file merge problem.

Chapter 9

The Two File Merge

One of the most difficult challenges in learning a programming technique is the two file merge problem. We will take on this problem in this chapter. In our example we will have two input files. The first file will be the master file whose FD and working storage are as follows:

```
FD  110-MASTER-FILE
    BLOCK CONTAINS 0 RECORDS
    RECORD CONTAINS 38 CHARACTERS
    RECORDING MODE IS F
    LABEL RECORDS ARE STANDARD
    DATA RECORD IS 110-MASTER-RECORD.
01  110-MASTER-RECORD   PIC X(38).

01  910-INPUT-AREA.
    05  910-EMPLOYEE-NBR    PIC X(05) VALUE SPACES.
    05  910-EMPLOYEE-NAME   PIC X(30) VALUE SPACES.
    05  910-COMMISSION-PCT  PIC 9(03) VALUE ZEROES.
```

The second file is the transaction file, whose FD and working storage are as follows:

```
FD  120-TRANS-FILE
    BLOCK CONTAINS 0 RECORDS
    RECORD CONTAINS 12 CHARACTERS
```

```
    RECORDING MODE IS F
    LABEL RECORDS ARE STANDARD
    DATA RECORD IS 120-TRANS-RECORD.
01  120-TRANS-RECORD   PIC X(12).

01  920-INPUT-AREA.
    05  920-EMPLOYEE-NBR   PIC X(05)    VALUE SPACES.
    05  920-TOTAL-SALES    PIC 9(05)V99 VALUE SPACES.
```

The program requirements are as follows. Match the incoming transaction records to the master file, and produce a transaction report. On a match compute the commission amount, write out the transaction report line, and produce a file to be sent to the payroll department. If an employee has no transaction records the program will produce a line on the error report showing the message "NO SALES FOR THIS EMPLOYEE". If a transaction record is found without an employee record the program will produce an error report line with the message "EMPLOYEE NUMBER NOT FOUND". We can now build the report definition:

```
****************************************************************************************
*** AREA DEFINES THE TRANSACTION REPORT LAYOUT                                    ***
****************************************************************************************
01  610-TRANSACTION-REPORT.
    05  610-LINE-COUNTER        PIC 9(03) VALUE ZEROES.
    05  610-PAGE-COUNTER        PIC 9(03) VALUE ZEROES.
    05  610-LINE-LIMIT          PIC 9(03) VALUE ZEROES.
    05  611-HEADER-LINE-1.
        .
        .
        .
    05  614-DETAIL-HEADER-LINE.
        .
        .
        .
    05  615-DETAIL-LINE.
        07  FILLER              PIC X(05)    VALUE SPACES.
        07  615-EMPLOYEE-NBR    PIC X(05)    VALUE SPACES.
```

```
07 FILLER                    PIC X(02)      VALUE SPACES.
07 615-EMPLOYEE-NAME         PIC X(30)      VALUE SPACES.
07 FILLER                    PIC X(02)      VALUE SPACES.
07 615-COMMISSION-PCT        PIC ZZ9        VALUE ZEROES.
07 FILLER                    PIC X(02)      VALUE SPACES.
07 615-TOTAL-SALES           PIC ZZZZ9.99   VALUE SPACES.
07 FILLER                    PIC X(02)      VALUE SPACES.
07 615-COMMISSION-AMT        PIC ZZZZ9.99   VALUE SPACES.
07 FILLER                    PIC X(02)      VALUE SPACES.
07 615-MESSAGE               PIC X(20)      VALUE SPACES.
```

We will not document the rest of this report layout, or the control report in this chapter. We have seen these definitions before. Nor will we need to detail the report writing paragraphs. These will be similar to the ones we built for the basic program. We will simply copy them into this program. Then we just have to find the right place to put the PERFORM Y400-WRITE-REPORT-LINE statement. This is because the function of the report module is independent of the rest of the program, and functionally cohesive. We can then parse out the functions of this program.

1) read the master file
2) read the transaction file
3) match the records
4) compute the commission amount
5) load the transaction report line
6) write the transaction report

From which we can outline the main drive of the program:

```
MATCH-PROGRAM
        PERFORM A100-INITIALIZATION
        PERFORM X100-READ-MASTER-FILE
        PERFORM X200-READ-TRANS-FILE
        PERFORM B000-MAIN-PROCESS
            UNTIL 310-END-OF-MASTER-FILE-FLAG = 'Y'
                OR 310-END-OF-TRANS-FILE-FLAG = 'Y'
```

```
        PERFORM C000-EOF-PROCESS
           UNTIL 310-END-OF-MASTER-FILE-FLAG = 'Y'
             AND 310-END-OF-TRANS-FILE-FLAG = 'Y'
        PERFORM E000-TERMINATION.


***********************************************************************************
*** PROCESS WILL MATCH THE TWO FILES UNTIL ONE OF THE FILES***
*** IS COMPLETED.                                            ***
***********************************************************************************
B000-MAIN-PROCESS.
     EVALUATE TRUE
           WHEN 910-EMPLOYEE-NBR = 920-EMPLOYEE-NBR
                PERFORM B200-LOAD-REPORT-LINE
                PERFORM B300-COMPUTE-COMMISSION
                PERFORM Y400-WRITE-REPORT-LINE
           WHEN 910-EMPLOYEE-NBR < 920-EMPLOYEE-NBR
                PERFORM B400-CHECK-MASTER-FILE
                PERFORM X100-READ-MASTER-FILE
           WHEN 910-EMPLOYEE-NBR > 920-EMPLOYEE-NBR
                PERFORM B500-CHECK-TRANS-FILE
                PERFORM X200-READ-TRANS-FILE
     END-EVALUATE.


***********************************************************************************
*** PROC WILL LOOP THRU THE INCOMPLETE FILE UNTIL IT IS     ***
*** ALSO USED UP.                                           ***
***********************************************************************************
C000-EOF-PROCESS.
     EVALUATE TRUE
           WHEN 310-END-OF-TRANS-FILE-FLAG = 'Y'
                PERFORM C200-MASTER-FILE-ERROR
                PERFORM Y400-WRITE-REPORT-LINE
                PERFORM X100-READ-MASTER-FILE
           WHEN 310-END-OF-MASTER-FILE-FLAG = 'Y'
                PERFORM C300-TRANS-FILE-ERROR
                PERFORM Y400-WRITE-REPORT-LINE
                PERFORM X200-READ-TRANS-FILE
     END-EVALUATE.
```

In this example the main drive has been split into two separate units of work. The first unit of work is the normal processing while both files are available. The second unit of work is an error process when one of the files is used up. We can do this because the internal decision processes of the two functions are independent of each other.

In the B000-MAIN-PROCESS there will always be a master file record and a transaction file record available. The processing decisions are then always based on the values of the keys of the master file and the transaction file.

If the keys are equal, then we will process the match by building the output report and getting the next transaction record. If the master file key is the lesser of the two, then we will report on any master key error, and we will get the next master file record. If the transaction file key is the lesser of the two, then we will report on any transaction key error, and we will get the next transaction file record. Let's examine each of these paragraphs in detail.

```
***=========================================================***
*** PARA LOADS THE REPORT LINE WITH DATA FROM THE TWO     ***
*** INPUT FILES.                                          ***
***=========================================================***
B200-LOAD-REPORT-LINE.
    MOVE 'Y' TO 310-TRANS-FILE-RCD-USED
    MOVE 'Y' TO 310-MASTER-FILE-RCD-USED
    MOVE 910-EMPLOYEE-NBR        TO 615-EMPLOYEE-NBR
    MOVE 910-EMPLOYEE-NAME       TO 615-EMPLOYEE-NAME
    MOVE 910-COMMISSION-PCT      TO 615-COMMISSION-PCT
    MOVE ZEROES                  TO 615-COMMISSION-AMT
    MOVE 920-TOTAL-SALES         TO 615-TOTAL-SALES
    MOVE SPACES                  TO 615-MESSAGE.

***=========================================================***
*** PARA COMPUTES THE COMMISSION AMT AS THE PRODUCT OF THE***
*** TOTAL SALES MULTIPLIED BY THE COMMISSION PERCENT.     ***
***=========================================================***
```

```
B300-COMPUTE-COMMISSION.
    COMPUTE 330-COMMISSION-AMT
        = 910-TOTAL-SALES
        * 920-COMMISSION-PCT.

    MOVE 330-COMMISSION-AMT  TO 615-COMMISSION-AMT.


***========================================================***
*** PARA CHECKS IF THE TRANS FILE RECORD WAS USED, IF IT    ***
*** WAS NOT USED WE WILL WRITE OUT AN ERROR REPORT RCD.     ***
***========================================================***
B400-CHECK-MASTER-FILE.
    IF 310-MASTER-FILE-RCD-USED = 'N'
        MOVE 910-EMPLOYEE-NBR              TO 615-EMPLOYEE-NBR
        MOVE 910-EMPLOYEE-NAME            TO 615-EMPLOYEE-NAME
        MOVE 910-COMMISSION-PCT           TO 615-COMMISSION-PCT
        MOVE ZEROES                       TO 615-COMMISSION-AMT
        MOVE ZEROES                       TO 615-TOTAL-SALES
        MOVE 'NO SALES FOR THIS EMPLOYEE' TO 615-MESSAGE
        PERFORM Y400-WRITE-REPORT-LINE
    END-IF.


***========================================================***
*** PARA CHECKS IF THE TRANS FILE RECORD WAS USED, IF IT    ***
*** WAS NOT USED WE WILL WRITE OUT AN ERROR REPORT RCD.     ***
***========================================================***
B500-CHECK-TRANS-FILE.
    IF 310-TRANS-FILE-RCD-USED = 'N'
        MOVE 920-EMPLOYEE-NBR             TO 615-EMPLOYEE-NBR
        MOVE SPACES                       TO 615-EMPLOYEE-NAME
        MOVE ZEROES                       TO 615-COMMISSION-PCT
        MOVE ZEROES                       TO 615-COMMISSION-AMT
        MOVE 920-TOTAL-SALES              TO 615-TOTAL-SALES
        MOVE 'EMPLOYEE NUMBER NOT FOUND'  TO 615-MESSAGE
        PERFORM Y400-WRITE-REPORT-LINE
    END-IF.


************************************************************************
*** THIS AREA DEFINES THE UTILITY FILE ACCESS PARAGRAPHS          ***
************************************************************************
```

```
***==========================================================***
*** PARA HANDLES THE PHYSICAL READ OF THE MASTER FILE      ***
***==========================================================***
X100-READ-MASTER-FILE.
     READ 110-MASTER-FILE INTO 910-INPUT-AREA
          AT END MOVE 'Y' TO 310-END-OF-MASTER-FILE-FLAG.

     IF 310-END-OF-MASTER-FILE-FLAG = 'N'
          MOVE 'N' TO 310-MASTER-FILE-RCD-USED
     END-IF.


***==========================================================***
*** PARA HANDLES THE PHYSICAL READ OF THE TRANSACTION FILE ***
***==========================================================***
X200-READ-TRANS-FILE.
     READ 120-TRANS-FILE INTO 920-INPUT-AREA
          AT END MOVE 'Y' TO 310-END-OF-TRANS-FILE-FLAG.

     IF 310-END-OF-TRANS-FILE-FLAG = 'N'
          MOVE 'N' TO 310-TRANS-FILE-RCD-USED
     END-IF.
```

A similar process will occur on the C000-EOF-PROCESSING, where we can assume that the records to be processed will not have a match.

```
***==========================================================***
*** PARA WRITES OUT THE MASTER FILE ERROR                  ***
***==========================================================***
C200-MASTER-FILE-ERROR.
     MOVE 910-EMPLOYEE-NBR         TO 615-EMPLOYEE-NBR
     MOVE 910-EMPLOYEE-NAME        TO 615-EMPLOYEE-NAME
     MOVE 910-COMMISSION-PCT       TO 615-COMMISSION-PCT
     MOVE ZEROES                   TO 615-COMMISSION-AMT
     MOVE ZEROES                   TO 615-TOTAL-SALES
     MOVE 'NO SALES FOR THIS EMPLOYEE' TO 615-MESSAGE.
```

```
***===========================================================***
*** PARA WRITES OUT THE MASTER FILE ERROR                    ***
***===========================================================***
C300-TRANS-FILE-ERROR
    MOVE 920-EMPLOYEE-NBR               TO 615-EMPLOYEE-NBR
    MOVE SPACES                         TO 615-EMPLOYEE-NAME
    MOVE ZEROES                         TO 615-COMMISSION-PCT
    MOVE ZEROES                         TO 615-COMMISSION-AMT
    MOVE 920-TOTAL-SALES                TO 615-TOTAL-SALES
    MOVE 'EMPLOYEE NUMBER NOT FOUND' TO 615-MESSAGE.
```

In fact the loading of the two error report lines can be turned into utility paragraphs, which could be called from both the B000- and the C000- sections of the program.

We can see that while this solution is highly structured, it is still more complicated than it has to be. And imagine what would happen if the 920- file contained an individual sales record for each catalog number. Or even if it contained the individual sales records by catalog number, which would have to be accumulated.

We could also easily be required to add an additional file which included any customer credits for returned merchandise which would reduce the employee's total sales, and hence his commission amount. This complication comes about because the main drive paragraph is not an elemental unit of work. We can change the main drive paragraph to be an elemental unit of work by replacing the match logic with an internal sort. The sort record will look like this:

```
01 940-SORT-RECORD.
    05 940-RECORD-TYPE      PIC  X(02)  VALUE SPACES.
    05 940-EMPLOYEE-NBR     PIC  X(05)  VALUE SPACES.
    05 940-EMPLOYEE-NAME    PIC  X(30)  VALUE SPACES.
    05 940-COMMISSION-PCT   PIC  9(03)  VALUE ZEROES.
    05 940-TOTAL-SALES      PIC S9(05)  V99 VALUE ZEROES.
```

We can then define the main unit of work as follows:

LEVEL I
Process the input files and create the match report.

Input	• Master file
	• Transaction file
Process	• Read the master file and release each record to the sort.
	• Read the transaction file and release each record to the sort.
	• Sort the sort file.
	• Build the report from the sort file records.
Rules	• Create a report line when two records match.
	• Create a report line when Master file records are not used.
	• Create a report line when Transaction file records are not used.
Output	• Transaction report.

We can then parse out our elemental units of work as follows:

LEVEL II
Read the master file and release each record to the sort.

Input	• The master file records
Process	• Load the sort record from the master file record
Rules	• The sort record number is 01
Output	• The sort file

Read the transaction file and release each record to the sort.

Input	• The transaction file records
Process	• Load the sort record from the master file record
Rules	• The sort record number is 02
Output	• The sort file

Return records from the sort.

Input	•	The sort file.
Process	•	Parse all the records from the sort into working storage fields.
Rules	•	Process all of the records with the same employee nbr.
Output	•	Parsed data from the sort file.

Build the report from the sort file records.

Input	•	Parsed data from the sort file.
Process	•	Build the report from the parsed data.
Rules	•	Create a report line when two records match.
	•	Create a report line when Master file records are not used.
	•	Create a report line when Transaction file records are not used.
Output	•	The matching results report.

Translating this into COBOL we begin by building the main drive of the program:

```
MATCH-PROGRAM
       PERFORM A100-INITIALIZATION
       SORT SORT-FILE BY ASCENDING 290-RECORD-TYPE
                                   290-EMPLOYEE-NBR
            INPUT  PROCEDURE B000-INPUT-PROCEDURE
            OUTPUT PROCEDURE C000-OUTPUT-PROCEDURE.
       PERFORM E000-TERMINATION.


***********************************************************************************
*** PROC WILL READ EACH INDIVIDUAL FILE AND WILL RELEASE  ***
*** ITS CONTENTS TO THE SORT.                             ***
***********************************************************************************
 B000-INPUT-PROCEDURE.
       PERFORM B100-MASTER-FILE.
       PERFORM B200-TRANSACTION-FILE.
```

```
***======================================================***
*** PROC READS EACH MASTER FILE RECORD AND RELEASES IT TO***
*** THE SORT.                                            ***
***======================================================***
 B100-MASTER-FILE.
    PERFORM X100-READ-MASTER-FILE
    PERFORM UNTIL 310-END-OF-MASTER-FILE-FLAG = 'Y'
        MOVE '01'                  TO 940-RECORD-TYPE
        MOVE 910-EMPLOYEE-NBR      TO 940-EMPLOYEE-NBR
        MOVE 910-EMPLOYEE-NAME     TO 940-EMPLOYEE-NAME
        MOVE 910-COMMISSION-PCT    TO 940-COMMISSION-PCT
        MOVE ZEROES                TO 940-TOTAL-SALES
        PERFORM X300-RELEASE-SORT-RECORD
        PERFORM X100-READ-MASTER-FILE
    END-PERFORM.


***======================================================***
*** PROC READS EACH TRANSACTION FILE RECORD AND RELEASES ***
*** IT TO THE SORT.                                      ***
***======================================================***
 B200-TRANSACTION-FILE.
    PERFORM X200-READ-TRANS-FILE
    PERFORM UNTIL 310-END-OF-TRANS-FILE-FLAG  = 'Y'
        MOVE '02'                  TO 940-RECORD-TYPE
        MOVE 920-EMPLOYEE-NBR      TO 940-EMPLOYEE-NBR
        MOVE SPACES                TO 940-EMPLOYEE-NAME
        MOVE ZEROES                TO 940-COMMISSION-PCT
        MOVE 920-TOTAL-SALES       TO 940-TOTAL-SALES
        PERFORM X300-RELEASE-SORT-RECORD
        PERFORM X200-READ-CREDIT-FILE
    END-PERFORM.


*******************************************************************
*** PROCESS WILL READ IN THE SORT FILE AND WILL PRODUCE    ***
*** THE OUTPUT REPORT.                                     ***
*******************************************************************

 C000-OUTPUT-PROCEDURE.
    PERFORM X400-RETURN-SORT-RECORD.
    PERFORM UNTIL 310-END-OF-SORT-FILE = 'Y'
```

```
        PERFORM C100-PARSE-SORT-FILE
        PERFORM C200-BUILD-REPORT
    END-PERFORM.


***========================================================***
*** PROC WILL READ EACH OF THE SORT RECORDS FOR AN EMPLOYEE***
*** AND WILL PARSE THE DATA TO THE WORKING STORAGE FIELDS.***
***========================================================***
C100-PARSE-SORT-FILE.
    PERFORM C110-INITIALIZE-THE-LOOP.
    PERFORM UNTIL 940-EMPLOYEE-NBR NOT = 440-EMPLOYEE-NBR
        EVALUATE TRUE
            WHEN 940-RECORD-TYPE = '01'
                PERFORM C120-SAVE-MASTER-RCD
            WHEN 940-RECORD-TYPE = '02'
                PERFORM C130-SAVE-TRANS-RCD
        END-EVALUATE
        PERFORM X400-RETURN-SORT-RECORD
    END-PERFORM.


***_____***
*** PROC INITIALIZES THE OUTPUT WORKING STORAGE FIELDS   ***
***_____***
C110-INITIALIZE-THE-LOOP.
    MOVE 'N'                TO 310-MASTER-RCD-FOUND
    MOVE 'N'                TO 310-TRANS-RCD-FOUND
    MOVE 940-EMPLOYEE-NBR TO 440-EMPLOYEE-NBR
    MOVE SPACES             TO 440-EMPLOYEE-NAME.
    MOVE ZEROES             TO 440-COMMISSION-PCT.
    MOVE ZEROES             TO 440-TOTAL-SALES.


***_____***
*** PROC SAVES OFF DATA FROM THE MASTER RECORD           ***
***_____***
C120-SAVE-MASTER-RCD.
    MOVE 'Y'                    TO 310-MASTER-RCD-FOUND
    MOVE 940-EMPLOYEE-NAME   TO 440-EMPLOYEE-NAME
    MOVE 940-COMMISSION-PCT  TO 440-COMMISSION-PCT.
```

```
***_____***
*** PROC SAVES OFF DATA FROM THE TRANSACTION RECORD        ***
***_____***
C130-SAVE-TRANS-RCD.
        MOVE 'Y'                TO 310-TRANS-RCD-FOUND
        MOVE 940-TOTAL-SALES    TO 440-TOTAL-SALES.


***=============================================================***
*** PROC WILL BUILD THE OUTPUT REPORT FROM THE LOADED      ***
*** WORKING STORAGE FIELDS.                                ***
***=============================================================***
C200-BUILD-REPORT
      PERFORM C220-LOAD-REPORT-LINE
      PERFORM C230-COMPUTE-COMMISSION
      PERFORM Y400-WRITE-REPORT-LINE.


***=============================================================***
*** PARA LOADS THE REPORT LINE, AND POPULATES THE ERROR    ***
*** MESSAGE FROM THE MESSAGE CODES.                        ***
***=============================================================***
C220-BUILD-RPT-LINE.
        MOVE 440-EMPLOYEE-NBR        TO 615-EMPLOYEE-NBR
        MOVE 440-EMPLOYEE-NAME       TO 615-EMPLOYEE-NAME
        MOVE 440-COMMISSION-PCT      TO 615-COMMISSION-PCT
        MOVE ZEROES                  TO 615-COMMISSION-AMT
        MOVE 440-TOTAL-SALES         TO 615-TOTAL-SALES
        MOVE SPACES                  TO 615-MESSAGE.
        EVALUATE TRUE
        WHEN 310-MASTER-RCD-FOUND = 'N'
            MOVE 'NO SALES FOR THIS EMPLOYEE' TO 615-MESSAGE
        WHEN 310-TRANS-RCD-FOUND = 'N'
            MOVE 'EMPLOYEE NUMBER NOT FOUND' TO 615-MESSAGE
        END-EVALUATE.


***=============================================================***
*** PROC COMPUTES THE COMMISSION AMT AS THE PRODUCT OF THE***
*** TOTAL SALES MULTIPLIED BY THE COMMISSION PCT.          ***
***=============================================================***
C230-COMPUTE-COMMISSION.
```

```
COMPUTE 440-COMMISSION-AMT
    = 440-TOTAL-SALES
    * 440-COMMISSION-PCT.

MOVE 440-COMMISSION-AMT TO 615-COMMISSION-AMT.
```

From this example, we can see the advantages of building our programs along the lines of elemental units of work. We can expand on this by making a small change to the problem. Instead of the transaction file having total sales, suppose we change the transaction file to be the individual sales records by catalog number instead of total sales. The new input file layout would be as follows:

```
01 920-INPUT-AREA.
    05 920-EMPLOYEE-NBR   PIC X(05)     VALUE SPACES.
    05 920-CATALOG-NO     PIC X(06)     VALUE SPACES.
    05 920-TOTAL-SALES    PIC 9(05)V99 VALUE SPACES.
```

The B200 paragraph would be changed to populate the new sort fields. The layout of the sort record would changed as follows:

```
01 940-SORT-RECORD.
    05 940-RECORD-TYPE     PIC  X(02)     VALUE SPACES.
    05 940-EMPLOYEE-NBR    PIC  X(05)     VALUE SPACES.
    05 940-EMPLOYEE-NAME   PIC  X(30)     VALUE SPACES.
    05 940-COMMISSION-PCT  PIC  9(03)     VALUE ZEROES.
    06 940-CATALOG-NO      PIC  X(06)     VALUE SPACES.
    05 940-TOTAL-SALES     PIC S9(05)V99 VALUE ZEROES.
```

The biggest change would be to the C130- paragraph. This is because we will now load the individual transaction records into a table. The table definition would be as follows:

```
01 810-CATALOG-TABLE.
    05 810-SUB        PIC 9(03)     VALUE ZEROES.
    05 810-LOAD       PIC 9(03)     VALUE ZEROES.
```

```
    05  810-LIMIT              PIC  9(03)     VALUE 999.
    05  810-TABLE-ROW OCCURS 999 TIMES.
      07  810-CATALOG-NO    PIC  X(06)     VALUE SPACES.
      07  810-TOTAL-SALES   PIC S9(05)V99 VALUE ZEROES.


***_____***
*** PROC SAVES OFF DATA FROM THE TRANSACTION RECORD TO ***
*** AN INTERNAL TABLE FOR FUTURE PRINTING                 ***
***_____***
C130-SAVE-CREDIT-RCD.
      MOVE 'Y'                   TO 310-TRANS-RCD-FOUND
      ADD 1 TO 810-LOAD.
      ADD 940-TOTAL-SALES        TO 440-TOTAL-SALES
      I F  810-LOAD LESS THAN 810-LIMIT
      OR 810-LOAD EQUAL       810-LIMIT
         MOVE 940-CATALOG-NO   TO 810-CATALOG-NO  (810-LOAD)
         MOVE 940-TOTAL-SALES  TO 810-TOTAL-SALES (810-LOAD)
         MOVE 940-CREDIT-REASON TO 810-CREDIT-REASON(810-LOAD)
      ELSE
         PERFORM Z999-TABLE-OVERFLOW
      END-IF.
```

The printing of the total line does not change, and we can add PER-FORM C240-PRINT-DETAIL to the C200-paragraph.

```
***=========================================================***
*** PROC WILL WRITE THE TABLE OF DETAIL LINES TO THE REPORT ***
***=========================================================***
C240-PRINT-DETAIL.
      PERFORM VARYING 810-SUB FROM 1 BY 1
             UNTIL 810-SUB GREATER THAN 810-LOAD
        MOVE 810-CATALOG-NO (810-SUB) TO 650-CATALOG-NO
        MOVE 810-TOTAL-SALES(810-SUB)  TO 650-TOTAL-SALES
        PERFORM Y500-WRITE-DETAIL-LINE
      END-PERFORM.
```

With this model we can also easily add a file of credit records to our processing.

```
01 930-INPUT-AREA.
    05  930-EMPLOYEE-NBR    PIC  X(05)      VALUE SPACES.
    05  930-CATALOG-NO      PIC  X(06)      VALUE SPACES.
    05  930-TOTAL-SALES     PIC S9(05)V99 VALUE SPACES.
    05  930-CREDIT-REASON   PIC  X(20)      VALUE SPACES.
```

We would add another load paragraph to the sort input process:

```
***=========================================================***
*** PROC READS EACH TRANSACTION FILE RECORD AND RELEASES ***
*** IT TO THE SORT.                                      ***
***=========================================================***
B300-CREDIT-FILE.
      PERFORM X300-READ-CREDIT-FILE
      PERFORM UNTIL 310-END-OF-CREDIT-FILE-FLAG  = 'Y'
            MOVE '03'                  TO 940-RECORD-TYPE
            MOVE 930-EMPLOYEE-NBR   TO 940-EMPLOYEE-NBR
            MOVE SPACES                TO 940-EMPLOYEE-NAME
            MOVE ZEROES                TO 940-COMMISSION-PCT
            MOVE 930-TOTAL-SALES    TO 940-TOTAL-SALES
            MOVE 930-CREDIT-REASON TO 940-CREDIT-REASON
            PERFORM X300-RELEASE-SORT-RECORD
            PERFORM X300-READ-CREDIT-FILE
      END-PERFORM.


***_____***
*** PROC SAVES OFF DATA FROM THE CREDIT RECORD TO AN     ***
*** INTERNAL TABLE FOR FUTURE PRINTING                   ***
***_____***
C130-SAVE-CREDIT-RCD.
      MOVE 'Y'                   TO 310-TRANS-RCD-FOUND
      ADD 1 TO 810-LOAD.
      ADD 940-TOTAL-SALES       TO 440-TOTAL-SALES
      IF 810-LOAD LESS THAN 810-LIMIT
      OR 810-LOAD EQUAL   810-LIMIT
          MOVE 940-CATALOG-NO   TO 810-CATALOG-NO  (810-LOAD)
          MOVE 940-TOTAL-SALES  TO 810-TOTAL-SALES  (810-LOAD)
          MOVE 940-CREDIT-REASON TO 810-CREDIT-REASON(810-LOAD)
```

```
        ELSE
            PERFORM Z999-TABLE-OVERFLOW
        END-IF.
```

In this chapter we have seen how to simplify the standard two file match problem. We did this by converting the process into a series of steps which were as close to elemental units of work as we could make them. This in turn allows us to easily add more functionality to the program by plugging in other elemental units of work. In the next chapter we will use our elemental units of work to build a simple COBOL/CICS program.

Chapter 10

The Basic CICS Program

Another challenging COBOL program is the online CICS program. Yet if we consider it, we would find that a CICS program is really just a very short running batch program. The task:

1) is started, with the object module being loaded from the library into the CPU.

2) takes in certain information from CICS through the special EIB area.

3) takes in certain information from calling programs through the LINK-AGE SECTION.

4) reads the screen data into working storage, just as a batch program reads data from a file.

5) reads data from and writes data to the Temporary Storage Queue.

6) processes the data that is brought in from the screen.

7) writes the screen data from working storage to the user, just as a batch program writes report records.

8) ends, and its resources are released.

So the basic program that we have designed should work for a CICS/COBOL programming request. We can see that this is true by examining a small, stand alone, data entry program, written in CICS/COBOL.

This program will allow the user to

1) enter an account number, and have the program display the information from the database.
2) accept changes to the data, validating it against preprogrammed rules.
3) update the database if all of the edits are approved, and after the user has pressed the PF5 key.
4) end the program when the user presses the PF3 key.

We can begin our examination by defining the units of work for this small program.

Main Process
Input
- EIB control area
- User keyed data from the screen

Process
- Initialize the control fields
- Check to see if this is the initial program entry
- Check for the use of a valid control key
- Receive the screen from the user
- Edit the input data - account number
- Edit the input data - payment date
- Edit the input data - payment amount
- Update the database
- Process the control key request - enter
- Process the control key request - PF Key 3
- Process the control key request - PF Key 5
- If required, display the screen to the user

Rules
- Allowable control keys are Enter, PF Key 3, and PF Key 5

Output
- Updated database records
- Screen display returned to the user with a message
- That informs the user that the update was successful.

Initialize the control fields

Input • None
Process • Initialize the control fields to their default values
Rules • None
Output • Send Screen Flag = 'Y'
• Error Found   = 'N'
• Screen Message Line = spaces

Check to see if this is the initial screen

Input • Field EIBCALEN of the EIB control area
Process • Check the EIBCALEN value, and prepare an initialized screen for the user.
Rules • If EIBCALEN = 0, then the user just started this transaction
Output • The initialized screen.

Check for the use of a valid control key

Input • Field EIBAID of the EIB control area
Process • Check the value if the field, return an error message if the value is not acceptable.
Rules • Field value must be DFHPF3, DFHPF5, DFHENTER
Output • Error message on the screen

Receive the screen from the user

Input • Screen data using the receive command
Process • Issue the receive command
• Replace the underscores in unused fields with spaces rules
Rules • None.
Output • Formatted screen input data

Edit the input data—account number

Input	•	Account number from the screen
Process	•	Edit the account number, and check to see if it is on the database.
Rules	•	Account number must be numeric
Output	•	If invalid, highlight the field and display the message

Edit the input data—payment date

Input	•	Payment date from the screen
Process	•	Edit the payment date
Rules	•	Payment date must be numeric, and it must be a valid date
Output	•	If invalid, highlight the field and display the message

Edit the input data—payment amount

Input	•	Payment amount from the screen
Process	•	Edit the payment amount
Rules	•	Payment amount must be numeric
Output	•	If invalid, highlight the field and display the message

Update the database

Input	•	Edited data from the screen
Process	•	Update the fields on the database
Rules	•	None
Output	•	Updated database record

Process the control key request—enter

Input	•	Enter Key
Process	•	Display data from the database record
Rules	•	Record must be found on the database
Output	•	Displayed screen data

Process the control key request—PF Key 3

Input	•	PF Key 3
Process	•	Skip the display on the screen
Rules	•	None
Output	•	Command to exit the program

Process the control key request—PF Key 5

Input	•	PF Key 5
Process	•	Control the updating of the database record
Rules	•	None
Output	•	Command to update the database

If required, display the screen to the user

Input	•	Data to be displayed on the screen
Process	•	Fill in empty fields with underscores
	•	Send the screen using the 'SEND MAP' command
	•	Execute the CICS 'RETURN' command. Include the successful update message
Rules	•	The send map flag must be set to YES
Output	•	Command to update the database

Once we have parsed the program, we can identify those parts of the program that we can consider as overhead, or house keeping logic. These are functions that are common to many similar CICS/COBOL programs. In this example, we can see three common routines. The first is a routine to receive the map into the program. The second is the routine to send the map to the operator. And the third is the routine to highlight the field and display the message. We can now begin by building the main drive portion of our program.

```
****************************************************************************************
*** PROCEDURE DIVISION                                                            ***
****************************************************************************************
PROCEDURE DIVISION.
      PERFORM A1000-INITIALIZATION.
      EVALUATE TRUE
          WHEN EIBCALEN = ZERO
              PERFORM B0000-FIRST-TIME
          WHEN EIBCALEN > ZERO
              PERFORM V1000-VALIDATE-PFKEYS
              IF 310-EDIT-ERROR-FOUND = 'N'
                  PERFORM V2000-RECEIVE-SCREEN
                  PERFORM C0000-PROCESS-REQUEST
              END-IF
      END-EVALUATE

      IF 310-SEND-MAP = 'Y'
          PERFORM V3000-SEND-SCRN-AND-RETURN
      END-IF.
```

As in our basic program, we will begin by initializing our control fields. The 310-SEND-MAP flag is used to determine if we want to send a map to the user at the end of the process. The default value is 'Y' but will be set to 'N' if the user presses PF Key 3 to exit the program.

The 310-EDIT-ERROR-FOUND flag is used for two purposes. First it is used to avoid certain processes. If an edit error was found, we will use this flag to avoid doing the database update. The second use is to control which error is displayed on the message line. We only want to display the first error message, so if the flag has been set to 'Y' we will not move a new literal into the message line.

```
**********************************************************************************
*** PROC INITIALIZES THOSE WORKING STORAGE FIELDS THAT ARE***
*** USED THROUGHOUT THE APPLICATION.                      ***
**********************************************************************************
A1000-INITIALIZATION.
     MOVE 'Y'              TO 310-SEND-MAP.
     MOVE 'N'              TO 310-EDIT-ERROR-FOUND.
```

Just as we found overhead processing in the batch programs to handle our file IO, (read, write, release, return), we will find that we have overhead processing in a CICS program when we do screen processing. We will label these CICS overhead paragraphs with a V000 designation, the same way we labeled the X000- and Y000- paragraphs.

This will leave the C0000- paragraphs with just the processing that is unique to this program, and the B0000 paragraphs to set up the initial screen display.

When the program is started, CICS will set the EIBCALEN field to zero. When this value is passed to the program, it will execute the initial screen setup logic and then execute the send map and return logic.

```
**********************************************************************************
*** AREA HANDLES THE INITIAL SCREEN LOAD WHICH INCLUDES:   ***
***   1) SETTING THE MESSAGE TO: PLEASE ENTER FIRST ACCOUNT NO***
**********************************************************************************
B0000-FIRST-TIME.
     MOVE 'PLEASE ENTER FIRST ACCOUNT NO' TO SCREEN-MSG.
     MOVE -1                              TO SCREEN-ACCT-NO-LEN.
```

```
**********************************************************************************
*** AREA HANDLES THE PHYSICAL SEND SCREEN PROCESSING      ***
**********************************************************************************
V3000-SEND-SCREEN-AND-RETURN.
     MOVE 'SC23'              TO EIBTRNID.
     PERFORM V3100-SET-DEFAULTS.
```

```
        PERFORM V3200-SET-DATE-TIME.
        PERFORM V3300-SET-UNDERSCORE.
        PERFORM V3900-CICS-SEND-MAP.
        PERFORM V3900-RETURN-SC23.


***=========================================================***
*** PROC ENSURES THAT THE CURSOR IS ON THE ACCOUNT-NO IF IT  ***
*** HAS NOT BEEN ASSIGNED TO A SPECIFIC LOCATION BY AN EDIT CMD***
***=========================================================***
V3100-SET-DEFAULTS.
        IF SCREEN-MESS          = SPACES
            MOVE -1             TO SCREEN-ACCOUNT-NO-LEN
        END-IF.


***=========================================================***
*** PROC CONTAINS THE CICS CMDS THAT SET THE DATE TIME DISPLAY***
***=========================================================***
V3200-SET-DATE-TIME.
        EXEC  CICS
            ASKTIME ABSTIME (320-ABSOLUTE-TIME)
        END-EXEC.

        EXEC  CICS
            FORMATTIME ABSTIME  (320-ABSOLUTE-TIME)
            DATESEP('/') MMDDYY (SCRHEAD-DATE)
            TIME (SCRHEAD-TIME) TIMESEP
        END-EXEC.


***=========================================================***
*** PROC PLACES UNDERSCORES IN EMPTY FIELDS                  ***
***=========================================================***
V3300-SET-UNDERSCORE.
        IF SCREEN-ACCOUNT-NO  <= SPACES
          MOVE ALL '_' TO SCREEN-ACCOUNT-NO
        END-IF
        IF SCREEN-PAYMENT-DATE <= SPACES
          MOVE ALL '_' TO SCREEN-PAYMENT-DATE
        END-IF
        IF SCREEN-PAYMENT-AMT  <= SPACES
          MOVE ALL '_' TO SCREEN-PAYMENT-AMT
        END-IF.
```

```
***========================================================***
*** PROC HANDLES THE PHYSICAL CICS SEND MAP COMMAND        ***
***========================================================***
 V3800-CICS-SEND-MAP.
     EXEC CICS
        SEND MAP ('SCM2300')
          MAPSET ('SCM2300')
          FROM    (SCM2300O)
          ERASE
          CURSOR
     END-EXEC.


***========================================================***
*** PROC HANDLES THE PHYSICAL END OF PROCESS RETURN TRANS   ***
***========================================================***
 V3900-RETURN-SC23.
     EXEC CICS
        RETURN TRANSID    ('SC23')
                COMMAREA  (DFHCOMMAREA)
                LENGTH       (LENGTH OF DFHCOMMAREA)
                RESP          (320-RESPONSE-CODE)
     END-EXEC
     IF 320-RESPONSE-CODE        NOT = DFHRESP(NORMAL)
        MOVE 'SC01'                  TO 320-DUMP-CODE
        PERFORM Z9990-DUMP
     END-IF.
```

The execution of this logic will lead to the display of the following screen:

```
┌─────────────────────────────────────────────────────────────┐
│                                                               │
│  SC23                ENTER CUSTOMER PAYMENTS        05/03/96   │
│                                                     10:23:20   │
│                                                               │
│   ACCOUNT NO      _____   NAME _____  │
│                                                               │
│   PAYMENT DATE      _____                                   │
│                                                               │
│   PAYMENT AMOUNT  _____                                     │
│                                                               │
│                                                               │
│                                                               │
│                                                               │
│   PLEASE ENTER FIRST ACCOUNT NO                               │
│  =========================================================    │
│  PF KEYS  3=EXIT  5=UPDATE                                     │
│                                                               │
│                                                               │
└─────────────────────────────────────────────────────────────┘
```

At this point the user will type in the first account number and will press the enter key. The EIBCALEN will now be greater than zero, and we will execute the second half of the logic. We will begin by examining the entered function key.

```
***************************************************************************************
*** PROC ENSURES THAT A VALID PFKEY WAS USED BY THE OPERATOR ***
***************************************************************************************
V1000-VALIDATE-PFKEYS.
     EVALUATE TRUE
          WHEN EIBAID  = DFHCLEAR
              OR EIBAID  = DFHPA1
              OR EIBAID  = DFHPA2
                   PERFORM V1200-CAPTURE-CLEAR
          WHEN EIBAID  = DFHPF3
              OR EIBAID  = DFHPF5
              OR EIBAID  = DFHENTER
```

```
            CONTINUE
        WHEN OTHER
            PERFORM V1300-CAPTURE-INVALID-KEY
    END-EVALUATE.


***========================================================***
*** PROC RESTORES THE SCREEN AFTER THE CLEAR KEY WAS USED, AND***
*** THEN BUILDS THE ERROR MESSAGE BASED ON THE IDENTIFIED KEY ***
*** MSG 153—THE CLEAR KEY IS NOT VALID ON THIS SCREEN.      ***
*** MSG 154—THE PA1 KEY IS NOT VALID ON THIS SCREEN.        ***
*** MSG 155—THE PA2 KEY IS NOT VALID ON THIS SCREEN.        ***
*** THIS PROC IS SEPARATE BECAUSE THERE IS NO SCREEN DATA   ***
*** TO RECEIVE ON CLEAR, PA1, OR PA2.  PGM WILL ABEND IF THE ***
*** RECEIVE MAP WAS ISSUED.                                 ***
***========================================================***
V1200-CAPTURE-CLEAR.
    EVALUATE TRUE
        WHEN EIBAID = DFHCLEAR
            MOVE 'THE CLEAR KEY IS NOT VALID ON THIS SCREEN'
            TO SCREEN-MSG
        WHEN EIBAID = DFHPA1
            MOVE 'THE PA1 KEY IS NOT VALID ON THIS SCREEN'
            TO SCREEN-MSG
        WHEN EIBAID = DFHPA2
            MOVE 'THE PA2 KEY IS NOT VALID ON THIS SCREEN'
            TO SCREEN-MSG
    END-EVALUATE.
    MOVE -1  TO SCREEN-ACCOUNT-NO-LEN.
    MOVE 'Y' TO 310-EDIT-ERROR-FOUND.


***========================================================***
*** PROC DISPLAYS THE MESSAGE THAT AN INVALID PFKEY WAS USED. ***
***========================================================***
V1300-CAPTURE-INVALID-KEY.
    PERFORM V2000-RECEIVE-SCREEN.
    MOVE 'AN INVALID PFKEY WAS USED ' TO SCREEN-MSG
    MOVE -1 TO SCREEN-ACCOUNT-NO-LEN.
    MOVE 'Y' TO 310-EDIT-ERROR-FOUND.
```

If the operator pressed the clear or the PA keys, the program will set a message, send the screen, and wait until the next control key is pressed. We will not receive the screen because this would cause a CICS abend. If the operator pressed another invalid key, the program will receive the screen into the IO area, set the error message, and return the screen to the user. It will then again wait for the next control key to be pressed. If a legitimate key was used, we will also receive the screen and begin the normal processing. The screen receive function includes the following logic:

```
*******************************************************************************
*** AREA HANDLES THE PHYSICAL RECEIVE SCREEN PROCESSING  ***
*******************************************************************************
 V2000-RECEIVE-SCREEN.
     PERFORM V2100-RECEIVE-MAP.
     PERFORM V2200-CLEAR-UNDERSCORE-LEFT.
     MOVE SPACES                      TO SCRTRAIL-MESS.


***==========================================================***
*** PROC HANDLES THE CICS RECEIVE MAP COMMAND                ***
***==========================================================***
 V2100-RECEIVE-MAP.
     EXEC  CICS
         RECEIVE MAP     ('SCM2300')
                 MAPSET ('SCM2300')
                 INTO    (WS02-SCM2300)
     END-EXEC.


***==========================================================***
*** PROC REMOVES THE UNDERSCORES FROM THE EMPTY FIELDS.  ***
***==========================================================***
 V2200-CLEAR-UNDERSCORE-RIGHT.
     INSPECT SCREEN-ACCOUNT-NO   CONVERTING '_' TO SPACES.
     INSPECT SCR230-PAYMENT-AMT  CONVERTING '_' TO SPACES.
     INSPECT SCREEN-PAYMENT-DATE CONVERTING '_' TO SPACES.
```

Here we see that we have executed the CICS "RECEIVE MAP" command, and we have cleared the extraneous underscores from the fields. We have done this here because the underscores only relate to the user interface, but the rest of the COBOL program expects an empty field to be spaces. If we did not do this, every check for spaces in the program would contain an OR statement to check for underscores. By initializing the fields before processing, we can simplify the program.

We are now ready to examine the main process of our program. What we have done so far is very similar to a batch program with break points. In the batch program we:

1) read the first record.
2) initialize the break points.
3) read the second record.
4) check the break points.
5) process the second record.

This is very similar to what we have done in our CICS program. We will:

1) receive the first transaction from the user.
2) send the first screen.
3) receive the second transaction from the user, which consists of our first screen.
4) check the control keys.
5) process the screen request.

Thus our process screen request is similar to the main body of our basic program. Here we will process the data that belongs to the transaction screen, and respond to the PF KEY request, just as we process the data in an input record, and respond to an end of file, or a data driven, processing request.

```
B000-MAIN-DRIVE-BATCH.
    PERFORM B100-EDIT-INPUT.
    IF 310-EDIT-ERROR-FOUND = 'N'
        PERFORM B200-UPDATE-THE-DATABASE
    END-IF.
    PERFORM X100-READ-INPUT-FILE.

C000-MAIN-DRIVE-CICS.
    PERFORM C100-EDIT-INPUT.
    IF 310-EDIT-ERROR-FOUND = 'N'
        PERFORM C200-UPDATE-THE-DATABASE
    END-IF.
    PERFORM C300-PROCESS-PFKEY
    IF 310-SEND-MAP = 'Y'
        PERFORM V300-SEND-SCREEN-AND-RETURN
    END-IF.
```

We can now examine each of these functions. We will use the edit function to ensure that the data entered on the screen is valid before we place it on the database. When we build an edit routine, we should be aware of some operational rules:

1) editing should be done in the same order that a page is read. In English, this is from the top to down, reading each line from left to right.

2) it is best to examine as many fields as possible on each pass. This avoids the frustration for the operator of having to clear an error, hitting the function key, and then having to clear another error. This is like the old joke of opening a present, only to find another present box inside, which in turn has another present box inside it which in turn has... until you are down to a very small box. This may be funny Christmas morning, but not on Monday morning when you are trying to get some work done.

3) while all of the fields in error should be highlighted, the cursor should be placed on the first error encountered, and the error message should describe the error for this field.

4) the data format on the screen is often different than the format on the database. For example, a date field might be in month, day, and year order on the screen, but it might be stored in year, month, and day order on the database. Thus it is often a good idea to reformat this data during the edit routine, and save the results, so they can be used during the update routine. This saves having to do the conversion twice, once for the edit and once for the update.

```
*******************************************************************************
*** AREA EDITS THE INPUT DATA FIELDS                                      ***
*******************************************************************************
B3000-EDIT-INPUT.
    PERFORM B3100-INITIALIZE-EDIT.
    EVALUATE TRUE
        WHEN EIBAID = DFHENTER
            PERFORM B3200-EDIT-ACCOUNT-NO
        WHEN EIBAID = DFHPF4
            PERFORM B3200-EDIT-ACCOUNT-NO
            PERFORM B3300-EDIT-PAYMENT-DATE
            PERFORM B3400-EDIT-PAYMENT-AMT
    END-EVALUATE.

B3100-INITIALIZE-EDIT.
    MOVE SPACES TO 430-PAYMENT-DATE
    MOVE SPACES TO 430-PAYMENT-AMOUNT.

***=====================================================================***
*** PROC EDITS THE ACCOUNT NUMBER, WHICH MUST BE GREATER THAN ***
*** SPACES, NUMERIC, AND ON THE DATABASE.                     ***
***=====================================================================***
B3200-EDIT-ACCOUNT-NO.
    IF SCREEN-ACCOUNT-NO = SPACES
        MOVE ATTR-UNPROT-ALPH-BRT-MOD TO SCREEN-ACCOUNT-NO-ATTR
```

```
IF 310-EDIT-ERROR-FOUND = 'N'
   MOVE 'ACCOUNT NO MUST BE GREATER THAN SPACES'
        TO SCREEN-MSG
   MOVE -1 TO SCREEN-ACCOUNT-NO-LENGTH
   MOVE 'Y' TO 310-EDIT-ERROR-FOUND
END-IF
END-IF.


IF SCREEN-ACCOUNT-NO NOT NUMERIC
   MOVE ATTR-UNPROT-ALPH-BRT-MOD TO SCREEN-ACCOUNT-NO-LENGTH
   IF 310-EDIT-ERROR-FOUND = 'N'
      MOVE 'ACCOUNT NO MUST BE NUMERIC' TO SCREEN-MSG
      MOVE -1 TO SCREEN-ACCOUNT-NO-LENGTH
      MOVE 'Y' TO 310-EDIT-ERROR-FOUND
   END-IF
END-IF.

IF 310-EDIT-ERROR-FOUND = 'N'
   PERFORM X100-CHECK-ACCOUNT-CD
   IF SQLCODE GREATER THAN 0
      MOVE ATTR-UNPROT-ALPH-BRT-MOD
                         TO SCREEN-ACCOUNT-NO-LENGTH
      IF 310-EDIT-ERROR-FOUND = 'N'
         MOVE 'ACCOUNT NO IS NOT ON FILE' TO SCREEN-MSG
         MOVE -1 TO SCREEN-ACCOUNT-NO-LENGTH
         MOVE 'Y' TO 310-EDIT-ERROR-FOUND
      END-IF
   END-IF
END-IF.
```

Before we continue coding the rest of the edit routine, we need to note something in this example. Of the 30 lines of code in this paragraph, 20 deal with displaying the error message. And much of this code will be redundant if we have multiple error messages in the program.

Most of it can also be classified as housekeeping, and from our earlier discussion, we decided that all of the housekeeping should be moved from the main logic of the program. This is especially true as we continue our "small batch program" example. We should return the screen as we would write a report. The highlighting of individual fields is like writing individual report lines.

Therefore, we will set up a common paragraph which will be called each time a field is to be highlighted, in the same way that we set up and called an common paragraph whenever a report line was to be written. We will begin by defining an set of flags which will tell our highlighting routine which field to process. There will be one entry per screen field.

```
*****************************************************************************
*** FIELDS ARE USED IN THE ERROR MESSAGE BUILDING PROCESS    ***
*****************************************************************************
01  350-ERROR-MSG-FIELDS.
    05  350-MSG                 PIC  X(80) VALUE SPACES.
    05  350-ERROR-CODE          PIC  9(04) VALUE ZEROES.
    05  350-FIELD-NUMBER        PIC  9(03) VALUE ZEROES.
    05  350-FIELD-NUMBER-VALUES.
        07  350-ACCOUNT-NO      PIC  9(03) VALUE 001.
        07  350-PAYMENT-DATE    PIC  9(03) VALUE 002.
        07  350-PAYMENT-AMOUNT  PIC  9(03) VALUE 003.
```

Our common routine will then receive the field number and the message from the calling edit, and will process the highlighting request.

```
***=========================================================***
*** THIS AREA HANDLES THE SCREEN HIGHLIGHTING AND DISPLAY OF ***
*** THE ERROR MESSAGE.                                       ***
***=========================================================***
V4000-DISPLAY-MSG.
    IF 310-EDIT-ERROR-FOUND = 'N'
        MOVE 'Y' TO 310-EDIT-ERROR-FOUND
        MOVE 350-MSG TO SCREEN-MSG
        PERFORM V4300-SET-MSG-CSR
    END-IF.
    PERFORM V4400-HIGHLIGHT-FIELD.
```

```
***_____***
*** THIS IS THE FIRST ERROR THAT HAS BEEN ENCOUNTERED, THUS WE***
*** WILL PLACE THE CURSOR HERE AND WE WILL DISPLAY THE MESSAGE***
***_____***
 V4300-SET-MSG-CSR.
     EVALUATE 350-FIELD-NUMBER
         WHEN 350-ACCOUNT-NO
             MOVE -1 TO SCREEN-ACCOUNT-NO-LENGTH
         WHEN 350-PAYMENT-DATE
             MOVE -1 TO SCREEN-PAYMENT-DATE-LENGTH
         WHEN 350-PAYMENT-AMT
             MOVE -1 TO SCREEN-PAYMENT-AMT-LENGTH
     END-EVALUATE.


***_____***
*** PROC CAUSES THE SELECTED FIELD TO BE REVERSE VIDEO DISPLAY  ***
***_____***
 V4400-HIGHLIGHT-FIELD.
     MOVE ATTR-UNPROT-ALPH-BRT-MDT TO 330-ATTR
     EVALUATE 350-FIELD-NUMBER
         WHEN 350-ACCOUNT-NO
             MOVE 330-ATTR  TO SCREEN-ACCOUNT-NO-ATTR
         WHEN 350-PAYMENT-DATE
             MOVE 330-ATTR  TO SCREEN-PAYMENT-DATE-ATTR
         WHEN 350-PAYMENT-AMT
             MOVE 330-ATTR    TO SCREEN-PAYMENT-AMT-ATTR END-
     EVALUATE.

     MOVE HILIGHT-REVERSE-VIDEO TO 330-ATTR
     EVALUATE 350-FIELD-NUMBER
         WHEN 350-ACCOUNT-NO
             MOVE 330-ATTR    TO SCREEN-ACCOUNT-NO-HILIGHT
         WHEN 350-PAYMENT-DATE
             MOVE 330-ATTR    TO SCREEN-PAYMENT-DATE-HILIGHT
         WHEN 350-PAYMENT-AMT
             MOVE 330-ATTR    TO SCREEN-PAYMENT-AMT-HILIGHT
     END-EVALUATE.
```

This will allow us to rewrite our edit paragraph in either of the following formats, using independent IF statements, or a single EVALUATE statement.

```
***==========================================================***
*** PROC EDITS THE ACCOUNT NUMBER, WHICH MUST BE GREATER THAN ***
*** SPACES, NUMERIC, AND ON THE DATABASE.                    ***
***==========================================================***
B3200-EDIT-ACCOUNT-NO.
      MOVE 350-ACCOUNT-NO TO 350-FIELD-NUMBER
      IF SCREEN-ACCOUNT-NO = SPACES
          MOVE 'ACCOUNT NO MUST BE GREATER THAN SPACES' TO 350-MSG
          PERFORM V4000-DISPLAY-MSG
      END-IF.

      IF SCREEN-ACCOUNT-NO NOT NUMERIC
          MOVE 'ACCOUNT NO MUST BE NUMERIC' TO 350-MSG
          PERFORM V4000-DISPLAY-MSG
      END-IF.

      IF 310-EDIT-ERROR-FOUND = 'N'
          PERFORM X100-CHECK-ACCOUNT-CD
          IF SQLCODE GREATER THAN 0
              MOVE 'ACCOUNT NO IS NOT ON FILE' TO 350-MSG
              PERFORM V4000-DISPLAY-MSG
          END-IF
      END-IF.
```

```
***==========================================================***
*** PROC EDITS THE ACCOUNT NUMBER, WHICH MUST BE GREATER THAN ***
*** SPACES, NUMERIC, AND ON THE DATABASE.                    ***
***==========================================================***
B3200-EDIT-ACCOUNT-NO.
      MOVE 350-ACCOUNT-NO TO 350-FIELD-NUMBER
      EVALUATE TRUE
          WHEN SCREEN-ACCOUNT-NO = SPACES
              MOVE 'ACCOUNT NBR MUST BE GREATER THAN SPACES'
                                              TO 350-MSG
          PERFORM V4000-DISPLAY-MSG
```

```
    WHEN SCREEN-ACCOUNT-NO NOT NUMERIC
        MOVE 'ACCOUNT NBR MUST BE NUMERIC' TO 350-MSG
        PERFORM V4000-DISPLAY-MSG
    WHEN NONE
        PERFORM X100-CHECK-ACCOUNT-CD
        IF SQLCODE GREATER THAN 0
            MOVE 'ACCOUNT NBR IS NOT ON FILE' TO 350-MSG
            PERFORM V4000-DISPLAY-MSG
        END-IF
END-EVALUATE.
```

This type of processing is especially helpful in those shops where the messages are stored in a database. This allows all of the programs in a system to use the same wording for a message. Thus we would add the following paragraph:

```
***_____***
*** PROC GETS THE SCRIPTED MESSAGE FROM THE DATABASE     ***
***_____***
V4100-SET-MESSAGE.
    PERFORM X3100-READ-SYSTEM-MSG
    IF SQLCODE = +100
        MOVE 'ERROR CODE IS NOT DEFINED' TO SCRTRAIL-MESS
    ELSE
        MOVE SYST-ERROR-MSG-TXT        TO SCRTRAIL-MESS
    END-IF.
```

Which would change our edit paragraph as follows:

```
***=========================================================***
*** PROC EDITS THE ACCOUNT NUMBER, WHICH MUST BE GREATER THAN ***
*** SPACES, NUMERIC, AND ON THE DATABASE.                ***
*** MSG 181—ACCOUNT NBR MUST BE GREATER THAN SPACES      ***
*** MSG 182—ACCOUNT NBR MUST BE NUMERIC                  ***
*** MSG 183—ACCOUNT NBR IS NOT VALID                     ***
***=========================================================***
B3200-EDIT-ACCOUNT-NO.
    MOVE 350-ACCOUNT-NO TO 350-FIELD-NUMBER
```

```
EVALUATE TRUE
    WHEN SCREEN-ACCOUNT-NO = SPACES
        MOVE 181 TO 350-ERROR-CD
        PERFORM V4000-DISPLAY-MSG
    WHEN SCREEN-ACCOUNT-NO NOT NUMERIC
        MOVE 182 TO 350-ERROR-CD
        PERFORM V4000-DISPLAY-MSG
    WHEN NONE
        PERFORM X100-CHECK-ACCOUNT-CD
        IF SQLCODE GREATER THAN 0
        MOVE 183 TO 350-ERROR-CD
            PERFORM V4000-DISPLAY-MSG
        END-IF
END-EVALUATE.
```

We can now build our other edit paragraphs:

```
***=======================================================***
*** PROC EDITS THE PAYMENT DATE, WHICH MUST BE GREATER THAN ***
*** SPACES, NUMERIC, AND VALID TO THE COMMON DATE ROUTINE   ***
*** MSG 142—PAYMENT DATE MUST BE GREATER THAN SPACES        ***
*** MSG 143—PAYMENT DATE MUST BE NUMERIC                    ***
*** MSG 144—PAYMENT DATE IS NOT VALID                       ***
***=======================================================***
B3300-EDIT-PAYMENT-DATE.
    MOVE 350-PAYMENT-DATE TO 350-FIELD-NUMBER
    EVALUATE TRUE
        WHEN SCREEN-PAYMENT-DATE = SPACES
            MOVE 142 TO 350-ERROR-CD
            PERFORM V4000-DISPLAY-MSG
        WHEN SCREEN-PAYMENT-DATE NOT NUMERIC
            MOVE 143 TO 350-ERROR-CD
            PERFORM V4000-DISPLAY-MSG
        WHEN NONE
            PERFORM B3210-CALL-DATE-ROUTINE
            IF DATE-ROUTINE-RETURN GREATER THAN 0
            MOVE 144 TO 350-ERROR-CD
                PERFORM V4000-DISPLAY-MSG
            ELSE
              MOVE DATE-ROUTINE-OUTPUT TO 430-PAYMENT-DATE
```

```
            END-IF
      END-EVALUATE.


***=======================================================***
*** PROC EDITS THE PAYMENT AMT, WHICH MUST BE GREATER THAN  ***
*** SPACES, NUMERIC, AND VALID TO THE NUMERIC EDIT ROUTINE   ***
*** MSG 232—PAYMENT AMT MUST BE GREATER THAN SPACES          ***
*** MSG 233—PAYMENT AMT MUST BE NUMERIC                      ***
*** MSG 234—PAYMENT AMT IS NOT VALID                         ***
***=======================================================***
  B3400-EDIT-PAYMENT-AMT.
      MOVE 350-PAYMENT-DATE TO 350-FIELD-NUMBER
      EVALUATE TRUE
          WHEN SCREEN-PAYMENT-AMT = SPACES
              MOVE 232 TO 350-ERROR-CD
              PERFORM V4000-DISPLAY-MSG
          WHEN SCREEN-PAYMENT-AMT NOT NUMERIC
              MOVE 233 TO 350-ERROR-CD
              PERFORM V4000-DISPLAY-MSG
          WHEN NONE
              PERFORM B3410-CALL-EDIT-ROUTINE
              IF EDIT-ROUTINE-RETURN GREATER THAN 0
                  MOVE 234 TO 350-ERROR-CD
                  PERFORM V4000-DISPLAY-MSG
              ELSE
                  MOVE EDIT-ROUTINE-OUTPUT TO 430-PAYMENT-AMT
              END-IF
      END-EVALUATE.
```

In both of these routines the program calls a common routine that belongs to this institution. We will discuss subroutines in a later chapter. Both routines also use this opportunity to translate the data into the database format. This formatted data will be used in the database update step.

We do this step separately because of its inherent complexity. In some cases we may be updating multiple databases. In this case, we are only updating one. Also, many applications update the database when ever all of the edits are passed. Splitting out the update routine allows us to change to this function by simply changing or removing the PFKEY check.

```
********************************************************************************
*** PROC UPDATE THE ACCOUNT DATABASE RECORD.                           ***
********************************************************************************
B4000-UPDATE-DATABASE.
    IF 310-EDIT-ERROR-FOUND = 'N'
        IF EIBAID = DFHPF5
            PERFORM X200-UPDATE-DATABASE
        END-IF
    END-IF.
```

And then we can deal with any additional PF KEY processing:

```
********************************************************************************
*** AREA HANDLES THE SPECIFIC PFKEY PROCESSING REQUESTS      ***
********************************************************************************
B5000-PROCESS-PFKEY.
    IF 310-EDIT-ERROR-FOUND = 'N'
        EVALUATE TRUE
            WHEN EIBAID = DFHENTER PERFORM B5400-INIT-DISPLAY
            WHEN EIBAID = DFHPF3   PERFORM B5500-EXIT-REQUEST
            WHEN EIBAID = DFHPF5   PERFORM B5600-DISPLAY-UPDT
        END-EVALUATE
    ELSE
        EVALUATE TRUE
            WHEN EIBAID = DFHPF3   PERFORM B5500-EXIT-REQUEST
        END-EVALUATE
    END-IF.

***==================================================***
*** PROC CLEARS THE SCREEN INPUT FIELDS                 ***
***==================================================***
B5400-INIT-DISPLAY.
    MOVE SPACES                        TO SCREEN-PAYMENT-DATE
    MOVE SPACES                        TO SCREEN-PAYMENT-AMT
    MOVE ACCOUNT-NAME OF ACCOUNT-DBASE TO SCREEN-ACCOUNT-NAME.
```

```
***========================================================***
*** PROC CONTROLS THE EXIT FROM THE PROGRAM, AND JUMPS TO   ***
*** OTHER SCREENS.                                          ***
***========================================================***
B5500-EXIT-REQUEST.
     MOVE 'N' TO 310-SEND-MAP
     EVALUATE TRUE
          WHEN EIBAID = DFHPF3   PERFORM Y3200-RETURN-CICS
     END-EVALUATE.


***========================================================***
*** PROC CLEARS THE SCREEN TO AVOID A DUPLICATE UPDATE      ***
*** MSG 370—DATABASE HAS BEEN UPDATED                       ***
***========================================================***
B5600-DISPLAY-UPDT.
     MOVE SPACES                    TO SCREEN-PAYMENT-DATE
     MOVE SPACES                    TO SCREEN-PAYMENT-AMT
     MOVE SPACES                    TO SCREEN-ACCOUNT-NAME.
     MOVE SPACES                    TO SCREEN-ACCOUNT-NO.
     MOVE 350-NO-HIGHLIGHT          TO 350-FIELD-NUMBER
     MOVE 370                       TO 350-ERROR-CD
     PERFORM V4000-DISPLAY-MSG.
```

The program will end this pass with the display of the screen which is found in paragraph V3000-SEND-SCREEN-AND-RETURN. If we review our initial parsing, we can see how the paragraphs were assigned to the functions:

PARSED PROCESS	DONE IN PARAGRAPH
Initialize the control fields	A1000
Check to see if this is the initial screen	A2000
Check for the use of a valid control key	A3000
Receive the screen from the user	V2000
Edit the input data - account number	B3200
Edit the input data - payment date	B3300
Edit the input data - payment amount	B3400
Update the database	B4000
Edit and process the PFKEY request	B5000
Process the control key request - enter	B5400
Process the control key request - PF Key 3	B5500
Process the control key request - PF Key 5	B5600
If required, display the screen to the user	V3000

From this skeleton, we can see how easily we can add more fields to the screen, and where we can plug in the additional functions. We will do this in the next chapter.

Chapter 11

Expanding the CICS Program

In this chapter we will continue to look at the CICS program problem by making changes to our basic program. One of the major challenges in writing a CICS program is in handling the interfaces that start the task. In a batch COBOL program, the operating system starts the task based on the JCL. In a CICS program, the operating system starts the task because the operator keyed in the "Transaction ID" on the screen, another program requests the transaction be started by using a CICS command, or the operator hits a control key on the screen, and the current transaction is restarted from the top of the program.

Because of this we need to check two different control areas. The EIB-CALEN gives the size of the COMMON AREA passed to the program. If this value is zero, then the task was started by the user typing in the Transaction ID on the screen. The EIBTRNID gives the last transaction id that was executed. If this value is equal to the current transaction id, then this is the second or subsequent execution of the program. If the transaction id is different, then this is the first execution of this program, and it was started from a different program.

So we will change our little program to now be one that is started by a larger program. The larger program (which will have a transaction id of X100) will validate the account number, and will pass it to our data entry program (which will have a transaction id of X110).

We will also check to see if the EIBCALEN is zero, and if it is we will have the program start a main menu program (transaction id X000). We will change the main drive of our program to look like this:

```
****************************************************************************************
*** PROCEDURE DIVISION                                                             ***
****************************************************************************************
PROCEDURE DIVISION.
    PERFORM A1000-INITIALIZATION.
    EVALUATE TRUE
        WHEN EIBCALEN    = ZERO
            PERFORM A2000-START-MENU
        WHEN EIBTRNID NOT = 330-TRANS-ID-LIT
            PERFORM B0000-FIRST-TIME
        WHEN EIBTRNID    = 330-TRANS-ID-LIT
            PERFORM V1000-VALIDATE-PFKEYS
            IF 310-EDIT-ERROR-FOUND = 'N'
                PERFORM V2000-RECEIVE-SCREEN
                PERFORM C0000-PROCESS-REQUEST
            END-IF
    END-EVALUATE.

    IF 310-SEND-MAP = 'Y'
        PERFORM V3000-SEND-SCREEN-AND-RETURN
    END-IF.
```

In this example, we can see that we have retained the same basic structure as in our original program. The only thing that we have changed is to check the EIBTRNID instead of the EIBCALEN in the second half of the EVALUATE statement. We then added the paragraph A2000-START-MENU, which contains a CICS START command.

```
***_____***
*** PROC DOES THE PHYSICAL STARTUP OF THE MAIN MENU PROGRAM ***
*** IF THE OPERATOR ENTERED THIS TRANSACTION FROM CICS.      ***
***_____***
A2000-START-MENU.
    EXEC CICS
```

```
        START
        TRANSID ('X000')
        TERMID  (EIBTRMID)
        RESP        (320-RESPONSE-CODE)
    END-EXEC.

    EXEC CICS
        RETURN
    END-EXEC.
```

However, the argument can be made that having a paragraph that executes a CICS command that starts another program (START, XCTL) violates the single entry/single exit rule. This is a valid argument because the system will stop processing this program as soon as it hits the A2000 paragraph, thus exiting the program early. To avoid this problem we could change the last paragraph as follows, and replace the A2000 paragraph:

```
    IF 310-SEND-MAP = 'Y'
        PERFORM V3000-SEND-SCREEN-AND-RETURN
    ELSE
        PERFORM V6000-CHANGE-TRANSACTIONS
    END-IF.
```

```
***=====================================================***
*** PROC SETS THE TRANSACTION ID SO THAT THE PGM WILL START  ***
*** THE MAIN MENU PROGRAM.                                   ***
***=====================================================***
 A2000-START-MENU.
        MOVE 'CICS' TO 330-NEXT-TRANS.
        MOVE 'N'   TO 310-SEND-MAP.
```

We will also add the following paragraphs:

```
***=====================================================***
*** PROC CONTROLS THE PROCESS OF STARTING THE NEXT          ***
*** TRANSACTION                                             ***
***=====================================================***
```

```
V6000-CHANGE-TRANSACTIONS.
    EVALUATE TRUE
        WHEN 330-NEXT-TRANS = 'X000' PERFORM V6100-START-X000
        WHEN 330-NEXT-TRANS = 'X100' PERFORM V6200-XCTL-X100
        WHEN 330-NEXT-TRANS = 'CICS' PERFORM V6300-RETURN-CICS
    END-EVALUATE.


***_____***
*** PROC DOES THE PHYSICAL STARTUP OF THE MAIN MENU PROGRAM ***
***_____***
V6100-START-X000.
    EXEC CICS
        START
        TRANSID ('X000')
        TERMID  (EIBTRMID)
        RESP    (320-RESPONSE-CODE)
    END-EXEC.

    EXEC CICS
        RETURN
    END-EXEC.
```

We can do this because we know that the program will need to either send the screen to the user, or to transfer control to CICS or another transaction. This allows us to restore the program to the single entry/single exit standard.

One of the advantages of having our program called as a subroutine is to be able to use the DFHCOMMAREA which is stored in the LINKAGE SECTION of the program. This area passed data from the starting program in much the same way that data is passed to a batch program on the EXEC card. This data be available to each execution of the program.

Another way to store data that is specific to each transaction is to use the CICS temporary storage queue. Suppose that we added a "REFRESH" function to our program that, when the user presses PF9, the program will display the previous version of the screen. To do this we need to save the screen image out to the temporary storage queue. This process will be added to the send map routine.

```
***_____***
*** FIELDS DEFINE THE TEMPORARY STORAGE QUEUE AREA.     ***
***_____***

01 950-TSQUEUE-AREA.
    05 950-SCRN-IMAGE     PIC X(1920).
    05 950-LAST-KEY-USED  PIC X(0005).
    05 950-DELETE-STATUS  PIC X(0001).


***_____***
*** PROC SAVES OFF THE SCREEN IMAGE TO THE TEMPORARY STORAGE ***
*** QUEUE.                                              ***
***_____***

V3500-SAVE-TSQUEUE.
    PERFORM Y5100-DELETE-TS-QUEUE.
    MOVE SCREENO                 TO 950-SCREEN-IMAGE
    MOVE 330-KEY-USED            TO 950-LAST-KEY-USED
    PERFORM Y5200-WRITE-TS-QUEUE.


***_____***
*** PROC DELETES THE REQUESTED TSQUEUE RECORD           ***
***_____***

Y5100-DELETE-TS-QUEUE.
    EXEC CICS
      DELETEQ TS
        QUEUE  (320-LAST-SCREEN-QUEUE)
        RESP   (320-RESPONSE-CODE)
    END-EXEC
    IF 320-RESPONSE-CODE = DFHRESP(NORMAL)
    OR 320-RESPONSE-CODE = DFHRESP(QIDERR)
      NEXT SENTENCE
    ELSE
      MOVE '0014'                TO 320-DUMP-CODE
      PERFORM Z9990-DUMP
    END-IF.


***_____***
*** PROC HANDLES THE WRITE TSQUEUE PROCESS              ***
***_____***

Y5200-WRITE-TS-QUEUE.
```

```
EXEC CICS
    WRITEQ TS
        QUEUE      (320-LAST-SCREEN-QUEUE)
        FROM       (950-TSQUEUE-AREA)
        LENGTH     (LENGTH OF 950-TSQUEUE-AREA)
        RESP       (320-RESPONSE-CODE)
END-EXEC
IF 320-RESPONSE-CODE    NOT = DFHRESP(NORMAL)
    MOVE '0015'                TO  320-DUMP-CODE
    PERFORM Z9990-DUMP
END-IF.
```

We will use the "last key" and the delete status fields later in this chapter. Now that we have saved off the last image, we can add the PF KEY 9 function to the program.

```
***********************************************************************************
*** AREA HANDLES THE SPECIFIC PFKEY PROCESSING REQUESTS   ***
***********************************************************************************
C5000-PROCESS-PFKEY.
    IF 310-EDIT-ERROR-FOUND = 'N'
        EVALUATE TRUE
            WHEN EIBAID = DFHPF3   PERFORM C5500-EXIT-REQUEST
            WHEN EIBAID = DFHPF5   PERFORM C5600-DISPLAY-UPDT
            WHEN EIBAID = DFHPF9   PERFORM C5900-REFRESH-SCRN
        END-EVALUATE
    ELSE
        EVALUATE TRUE
            WHEN EIBAID = DFHPF3   PERFORM C5500-EXIT-REQUEST
            WHEN EIBAID = DFHPF9   PERFORM C5900-REFRESH-SCRN
        END-EVALUATE
    END-IF.


***=====================================================***
*** PROC CONTROLS THE EXIT FROM THE PROGRAM             ***
***=====================================================***
C5500-EXIT-REQUEST.
    MOVE 'N' TO 310-SEND-MAP
    EVALUATE TRUE
```

```
           WHEN EIBAID = DFHPF3   MOVE 'X100' TO 330-NEXT-TRANS
           END-EVALUATE.


***========================================================***
*** PROC CLEARS THE SCREEN TO AVOID A DUPLICATE UPDATE   ***
*** MSG 370—DATABASE HAS BEEN UPDATED                    ***
***========================================================***
C5600-DISPLAY-UPDT.
       MOVE SPACES                      TO SCREEN-PAYMENT-DATE
       MOVE SPACES                      TO SCREEN-PAYMENT-AMT
       MOVE 350-NO-HIGHLIGHT            TO 350-FIELD-NUMBER
       MOVE 370                         TO 350-ERROR-CD
       PERFORM V4000-DISPLAY-MSG.
```

First we should note the changes that were made to this part of the program based on our earlier discussion. The C5500-paragraph has been changed to set the 330-NEXT-TRANS field instead performing the paragraph to return to the calling program. This again returns the program to the single entry/single exit standard. We also eliminated the C5400-paragraph because the ENTER key is no longer valid, and we stopped clearing the account number and name data on the update.

These changes are easier to make because the module programming kept each function separate. Thus we only had to delete a few lines of code. And now we can add our new refresh function.

```
***========================================================***
*** PROC HANDLES THE REFRESH SCREEN REQUEST.             ***
*** MSG 199—SCRN HAS BEEN REFRESHED PER THE USER REQUEST ***
***========================================================***
C5900-REFRESH-SCRN.
       PERFORM Y5300-READ-TS-QUEUE.
       MOVE 950-SCREEN-IMAGE            TO SCREENO
       MOVE 350-NO-HIGHLIGHT            TO 350-FIELD-NUMBER
       MOVE 199                         TO 350-ERROR-CD
       PERFORM V4000-DISPLAY-MSG.
```

```
***_____***
*** PROC READS THE REQUESTED TSQUEUE RECORD          ***
***_____***
Y5300-READ-TS-QUEUE.
      EXEC CICS
         READQ TS
            QUEUE    (320-LAST-SCREEN-QUEUE)
            INTO     (950-TSQUEUE-AREA)
            ITEM     (+1)
            RESP     (320-RESPONSE-CODE)
      END-EXEC
      IF 320-RESPONSE-CODE       NOT = DFHRESP(NORMAL)
         MOVE '0016'          TO  320-DUMP-CODE
         PERFORM Z9990-DUMP
      END-IF.
```

Now that we have the screen image saved, we can use it in other places. For example, in the case where the user pressed the clear key, we could restore the image of the last displayed screen, and then append the message to it.

```
***==========================================================***
*** PROC RESTORES THE SCREEN AFTER THE CLEAR KEY WAS USED,    ***
*** AND THEN BUILDS THE ERROR MESSAGE BASED ON THE            ***
*** IDENTIFIED KEY                                            ***
*** MSG 153—THE CLEAR KEY IS NOT VALID ON THIS SCREEN         ***
*** MSG 154—THE PA1 KEY IS NOT VALID ON THIS SCREEN.          ***
*** MSG 155—THE PA2 KEY IS NOT VALID ON THIS SCREEN.          ***
*** THIS PROC IS SEPARATE BECAUSE THERE IS NO SCREEN DATA     ***
*** TO RECEIVE ON CLEAR, PA1, OR PA2.  PGM WILL ABEND IF      ***
*** THE RECEIVE MAP WAS ISSUED.                               ***
***==========================================================***
V1200-CAPTURE-CLEAR.
      PERFORM Y5300-READ-TS-QUEUE.
      MOVE 950-SCREEN-IMAGE        TO SCREENO
      EVALUATE TRUE
         WHEN EIBAID = DFHCLEAR
               MOVE 'THE CLEAR KEY IS NOT VALID ON THIS SCREEN'
               TO SCREEN-MSG
```

```
          WHEN EIBAID = DFHPA1
              MOVE 'THE PA1 KEY IS NOT VALID ON THIS SCREEN'
              TO SCREEN-MSG
          WHEN EIBAID = DFHPA2
              MOVE 'THE PA2 KEY IS NOT VALID ON THIS SCREEN'
              TO SCREEN-MSG
      END-EVALUATE.
      MOVE -1  TO SCREEN-ACCOUNT-NO-LEN.
      MOVE 'Y' TO 310-EDIT-ERROR-FOUND.
```

We could also use the screen image on a return from another program, such as a help screen.

```
*************************************************************************************
*** PROCEDURE DIVISION                                                          ***
*************************************************************************************
PROCEDURE DIVISION.
    PERFORM A1000-INITIALIZATION.
    EVALUATE TRUE
        WHEN EIBCALEN     = ZERO
            PERFORM A2000-START-MENU
        WHEN EIBTRNID NOT = 330-TRANS-ID-LIT
            PERFORM B0000-FIRST-TIME
        WHEN EIBTRNID     = 330-TRANS-ID-LIT
            PERFORM V1000-VALIDATE-PFKEYS
            IF 310-EDIT-ERROR-FOUND = 'N'
                PERFORM V2000-RECEIVE-SCREEN
                PERFORM C0000-PROCESS-REQUEST
            END-IF
    END-EVALUATE.

    IF 310-SEND-MAP = 'Y'
        PERFORM V3000-SEND-SCREEN-AND-RETURN
    ELSE
        PERFORM V6000-CHANGE-TRANSACTIONS
    END-IF.
```

```
**********************************************************************
*** PROC HANDLES THE PREPARATION FOR THE FIRST DISPLAY OF  ***
*** THE SCREEN.  IF WE ARE RETURNING FROM THE HELP SCREEN,  ***
*** THEN WE WILL RETRIEVE THE SCREEN IMAGE FROM THE TEMP  ***
*** STORAGE QUEUE.                                           ***
**********************************************************************
B0000-FIRST-TIME.
    IF EIBTRNID = 'H100'
       PERFORM Y5300-READ-TS-QUEUE
       MOVE 950-SCREEN-IMAGE          TO SCREENO
    ELSE
       MOVE DFHCOMM-ACCOUNT-NO   TO SCREEN-ACCOUNT-NO
       MOVE DFHCOMM-ACCOUNT-NAME TO SCREEN-ACCOUNT-NAME
    END-IF.
```

It can also be argued that since this read occurs in multiple places, it might be better if we moved it to the top of the program. The higher the read is placed in the program, the lesser the chance there is of either a duplicate read of the data, or of missing the read entirely. Thus we can add this initialization of the loop as follows:

```
**********************************************************************
*** PROC READS THE TSQUEUE AREA TO HAVE THE HELD DATA    ***
*** AVAILABLE TO THE PROGRAM.                             ***
**********************************************************************
A1100-READ-TSQUEUE.
    IF  EIBTRNID = 'H100'
    OR EIBTRNID = 'X110'
        PERFORM Y5300-READ-TS-QUEUE
    END-IF.
```

This way the data is available to the program whenever it is needed. However, we will not move the data until it is needed.

```
***=========================================================***
*** PROC HANDLES THE REFRESH SCREEN REQUEST.              ***
*** MSG 199—SCRN HAS BEEN REFRESHED PER THE USER REQUEST***
***=========================================================***
C5900-REFRESH-SCRN.
     MOVE 950-SCREEN-IMAGE          TO SCREENO
     MOVE 350-NO-HIGHLIGHT          TO 350-FIELD-NUMBER
     MOVE 199                       TO 350-ERROR-CD
     PERFORM V4000-DISPLAY-MSG.
```

Placing the read of the Temporary Storage Queue at the top of the program is a good example of the use of the Temporal Cohesion that we discussed in Chapter 3. This is especially true if the data on the record used is used in more than one place.

For example, if we changed the program to receive both the account number and the payment date from the starting program. We also added a delete function using PF KEY 4.

As in many delete functions, we want to give the user the chance to change their minds before the delete occurs. To do this we need to have the user press the PF KEY 4 key twice, which in turn means we need to know what the last key used was. We will store this last used key in the Temporary Storage queue.

```
***=========================================================***
*** PROC HANDLES THE REFRESH SCREEN REQUEST.              ***
*** MSG 405—PLEASE PRESS PFKEY 10 TO CONFIRM DELETE       ***
***=========================================================***
C5900-REFRESH-SCRN.
     EVALUATE TRUE
         WHEN 950-LAST-KEY  NOT EQUAL 'PFKEY10'
         AND 950-DELETE-STATUS EQUAL '1'
             MOVE '0'                    TO 950-DELETE-STATUS
             PERFORM X300-DELETE-RECORD
         WHEN 950-LAST-KEY     EQUAL 'PFKEY10'
```

```
            MOVE '1'                    TO 950-DELETE-STATUS
            MOVE 350-NO-HIGHLIGHT TO 350-FIELD-NUMBER
            MOVE 405                    TO 350-ERROR-CD
            PERFORM V4000-DISPLAY-MSG
        END-EVALUATE.
```

By reading the temporary storage queue at the top of the program, its multiple pieces of data are available through out the program.

Another example of this good temporal cohesion is found in our help routine. We could have a different help display screen for each field on the screen. This would require us to determine which field the cursor is on before calling the help routine (H100).

```
***======================================================***
*** PROC HANDLES THE HELP SCREEN REQUEST                  ***
***======================================================***
  C5100-HELP-ROUTINE.
        MOVE 'N'                    TO 310-SEND-SCREEN.
        MOVE 'H100'                 TO 330-NEXT-TRANS
        MOVE 360-CURSOR-FIELD-NO    TO H100-COMM-AREA-FIELD-NO.
```

This determination could either be done here, or as part of the receive screen routine. The author would put it in the receive screen routine because the cursor position could be helpful to other routines in the program, and thus could be thought of as a program level value. For example, if this program had both a help screen, and a cursor sensitive scrolling routine, both routines would need the cursor position. Since both routines are dependent on the value of the cursor field, the routine to determine it should be placed above each routine. Since it changes each time the screen is changed, then it should be part of the receive screen routine.

```
***======================================================***
*** THESE FIELDS ARE USED TO CALL SCRPOSIT AND THEN TO    ***
*** SELECT WHICH FIELD THE CURSOR IS IN.                  ***
***======================================================***
```

```
01 360-FIELD-NUM-CURSOR-AREA.
   05 360-CURSOR-RECVD-FLD   PIC  9(02) VALUE ZEROES.
   05 360-CURSOR-RECVD-ROW   PIC  9(02) VALUE ZEROES.
   05 360-CURSOR-RECVD-COL   PIC  9(02) VALUE ZEROES.
   05 360-ROW-POSIT               PIC  9(02) VALUE ZEROES.
      88 360-COL-ACCOUNT-NO              VALUE 04.
      88 360-COL-PAYMENT-DATE            VALUE 06.
      88 360-COL-PAYMENT-AMT             VALUE 08.
   05 360-COLUMN-POSIT            PIC  9(02) VALUE ZEROES.
      88 360-COL-ACCOUNT-NO              VALUE 18 THRU 26.
      88 360-COL-PAYMENT-DATE            VALUE 22 THRU 26.
      88 360-COL-PAYMENT-AMT             VALUE 20 THRU 26.


***=========================================================***
*** PROC HANDLES THE HELP SCREEN REQUEST                   ***
***=========================================================***
V2300-FIND-CURSOR.
     PERFORM V2310-CALL-SCRPOSIT
     PERFORM V2320-FIND-FIELD.


***_____***
*** PROC CALLS SCRPOSIT WHICH TRANSLATES THE IBM/CICS      ***
*** CURSOR POSITION TO A SET OF ROW/COLUMN COORDINATES.    ***
***_____***
V2310-CALL-SCRPOSIT.
     MOVE ZEROES TO 360-CURSOR-RECVD-FLD
     MOVE ZEROES TO 360-CURSOR-RECVD-ROW
     MOVE ZEROES TO 360-CURSOR-RECVD-COL

     CALL 'SCRPOSIT' USING EIBCPOSN
                     360-CURSOR-RECVD-ROW
                     360-CURSOR-RECVD-COL.

     MOVE 360-CURSOR-RECVD-ROW   TO 360-ROW-POSIT
     MOVE 360-CURSOR-RECVD-COL   TO 360-COLUMN-POSIT.


***_____***
*** PROC DETERMINES WHICH FIELD THE CURSOR IS IN.          ***
***_____***
```

```
V2320-FIND-FIELD.
    IF 360-ROW-ACCOUNT-NO     AND 360-COL-ACCCUTN-NO
        MOVE 350-ACCOUNT-NO       TO 360-CURSOR-RECVD-FLD.
    IF 360-ROW-PAYMENT-DATE   AND 360-COL-PAYMENT-DATE
        MOVE 350-PAYMENT-DATE     TO 360-CURSOR-RECVD-FLD.
    IF 360-ROW-PAYMENT-AMT    AND 360-COL-PAYMENT-AMT
        MOVE 350-PAYMENT-AMT      TO 360-CURSOR-RECVD-FLD.
```

In this example we use a subroutine to translate the CICS supplied cursor position. This value is the number of bytes from the top left hand side of the screen to the cursor position. The EIBCPOSN is translated into a cursor row and column, which in turn is used to identify the selected field.

We have seen a number of subroutines through these last two chapters. Subroutines are a important part of structured programming, and they are the subject of the next chapter.

Chapter 12

The Subroutine

When designing a system, we often find the need to code the same function for use in multiple applications. This can be done in different ways. The first method is to place the same code in each program that needs the function. The second method is to isolate the code in a unique module, which the other programs can access with a call routine. These isolated modules are called subroutines or subprograms. Subprograms can be defined as programs that are totally dependent on another program for execution. In COBOL this means that the execution of the program is started by a CALL or a CICS LINK command.

Subprograms are usually built to accomplish a single function. There are three advantages to using subroutines. First, subroutines can be used to isolate a particularly complicated piece of logic. For example, a sales tax computation routine could be isolated, allowing us to test it more easily by build a "test stand". This would be an online screen where we input specific parameters, and then view the results. This makes testing easier and more through because the input and the results are not filtered through the primary application.

The second advantage is that a subroutine will allow us to avoid redundant coding. For example, how many times would we want to code a date edit and conversion process. Putting this in a subprogram will allow us to remove housekeeping, logic from the main program, making it easier to understand.

The third advantage is that a subroutine can give us the same results across multiple applications. This would be particularly useful for a multi-step process that is used by several programs. An example would be a routine that retrieved and formatted an employee name for display on a screen. Using a subroutine to retrieve and format the name allows the display to be the same on every screen in the system.

The main disadvantage in using subprograms comes from the maintenance problems. It is often easier to debug a single, large, well written program, than it is to track a problem through a nest of subprograms. To avoid this problem we have to ensure that the rules of coupling and cohesion are applied to the structure of the program's subroutines. Each subroutine should be a functionally cohesive module. The order of execution of the subroutines should be controlled by a sequentially cohesive module.

We have seen examples of the use of subprograms in the last chapter. There we saw routines which converted the IBM supplied EIBCPOSN to a row and column location, handled the date edit request, converted the date to a new format, and handled the numeric edit request, and converted the input to a numeric value.

In this chapter we will discuss some rules for when and how to use a subprogram. The first consideration that we need to make is how many programs will use this particular routine. A commonly used routine, like the one to convert the EIBCPOSN is a perfect candidate for a subprogram, as many programs would use it. Conversely, it would be best to keep a simple algorithm that is used by a single program inside that program.

If the routine is used by just a few programs, then we also need to look at the size of the proposed subprogram. If this is complicated routine that we need to isolate, or a large routine that must give consistent results for different programs, then we can make a subprogram out of it. If the number of lines of actual logic is less than the number of lines of housekeeping logic, then it probably makes more sense to keep it in the main program.

However, the most important point in designing subprograms is to review the concept of "locality of reference". Locality of reference refers to how many modules are between the original source of a parameter value, and the subprogram that depends on that data. By their very nature, subprograms are effected by the level of program coupling.

What we want to do is to minimize the number of layers that a piece of data is passed through. For example, the author worked on one system where a module had the following subprogram hierarchy:

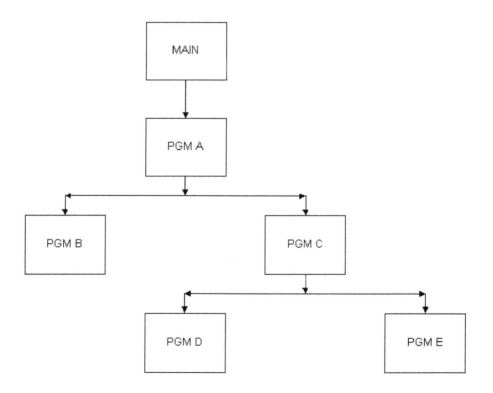

Figure 12.1

The purpose of this subprogram string was to retrieve the status of a traveler's check from the database. Programs B, D, and E were just database access programs, while programs A and C decided which program stream to call. Thus to find a missing piece of data in program E, one had to search programs A and C.

Again we want to make the structure of the called programs as level as possible. Thus if program C's functions were pulled into program A we would have the following structure.

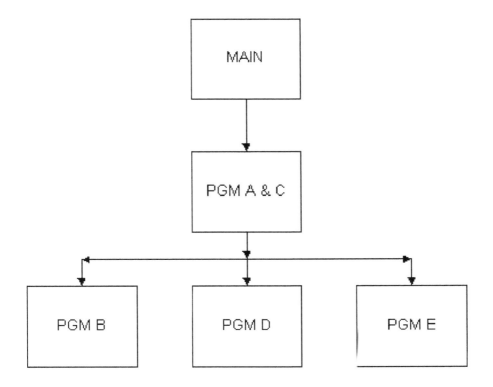

Figure 12.2

Or using a cascade diagram:

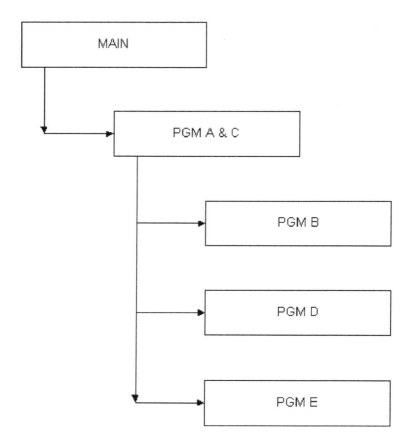

Figure 12.3

This of course eliminates one program level, and shortens the coupling path.

We must also look at which program controls the processing. For example, we could have a system where a series of historical processing dates may be entered on different screens. There are two ways to build a subprogram to handle this common edit.

One method is to handle the edit at the program level, where each program passes all of the fields at once. If a certain screen doesn't have that value then a dummy field must be passed. The unit of work for this subroutine would look like this:

Input	• Fields from input screen program in month, day, year format
	• Program ID of the calling program
Processing	• Edit FIELD-1, required, numeric, valid date
	• Edit FIELD-2, required, numeric, valid date
	• Edit FIELD-3, required, numeric, valid date
	• Edit FIELD-3, must be 10 days greater than FIELD-2
	• Edit FIELD-4, required, numeric, valid date
	• Edit FIELD-5, required, numeric, valid date
	• Edit FIELD-6, required, numeric, valid date
	• Edit FIELD-7, required, numeric, valid date
	• Edit FIELD-7, must be 30 days greater than FIELD-6
	• Convert each date to Year, month, day format
Rules	• FIELD-5 is not available to program 2.
	• FIELD-7 is not available to program 3.
Output	• Converted field values
	• Indicators to show which fields are in error
	• Error message code for each field in error

In this example, the program must examine the program id to determine if it should perform the edits for fields 5 and 7. The calling program must also decipher the indicators that are returned to determine which fields are in error.

The second method is to place the control in the calling program, and our subprogram will only edit one field at a time.

Input	•	Field from input screen program in month, day, year format
	•	Field ID of the input field
Processing	•	Apply edit rules to the input fields convert each date to Year, month, day format
Rules	•	Edit input FIELD, required, numeric, valid date
	•	FIELD-3 must be 10 days greater than FIELD-2
	•	FIELD-7 must be 30 days greater than FIELD-6
Output	•	Converted field values
	•	Error message code if the input field in error

In this example, the supplied field id determines which edits will be done. This is better because the field id relates directly to the edits to be done, rather than relying on the program id to control the processing.

Another example of the problem of determine the proper level of control can be seen in these units of work. These routines compute the sales tax amount.

Input	•	Tax rate from database
	•	Taxable amount
Processing	•	Apply the tax rate to the taxable amount
Rules	•	Tax amount is equal to the taxable amount multiplied by the tax rate.
Output	•	Tax amount

Input	•	Tax rate location
	•	Taxable amount
Processing	•	Obtain the tax rate for the input location from the database.
	•	Apply the tax rate to the taxable amount
Rules	•	Tax amount is equal to the taxable amount multiplied by the tax rate.
Output	•	Tax amount

In the first routine the calling program is responsible only for the multiplication process. In the second routine, the subprogram must obtain the tax rate from the database for the input location.

The second method is better because we only have to track back through one layer to find the source of the location. In the first routine we have to go outside the program to find both the source of the tax rate and the source of the location.

After we determine where the data is being passed from, we must also look at how much data is being passed. Again we want to minimize the amount of data that is passed back and forth from the main program to the subprogram. For example, we can have a routine that formats the name of a store owner. In one system this required:

1) reading the store record to get the social security numbers of the store owners on a particular date.
2) reading the store owner record for the primary owner.
3) reading the store owner record for the secondary owner.
4) formatting the names.

There are two different ways to approach this process. Either the calling program can read the store record and pass the required SSNs, of the calling program can simply pass the store number. We can see these two methods in the following parsing arrays.

1) The calling program passes the store number.

Input	•	Store number
Processing	•	Read the store record to get the SSN of the store owners.
	•	Read the store owner record for the primary owner.
	•	Read the store owner record for the secondary owner.
	•	Format the names, removes excess spaces
Rules	•	For a single owner, output is first-name last-name
	•	For multiple owners who are husband and wife, output is Primary Owners First Name, Secondary Owners First Name, and Primary Owners Last Name.
	•	For multiple owners who are not husband and wife, output is Primary Owners First and last Name, Secondary Owners First and Last Name.
Output	•	Store owner name display

2) The calling program passes the SSNs.

Input	•	SSN of primary store owner
	•	SSN of secondary store owner
Processing	•	Read the store owner record for the primary owner.
	•	Read the store owner record for the secondary owner.
	•	Format the names, removes excess spaces
Rules	•	For a single owner, output is first-name last-name
	•	For multiple owners who are husband and wife, output is Primary Owners First Name, Secondary Owners First Name, and Primary Owners Last Name.
	•	For multiple owners who are not husband and wife, output is Primary Owners First and last Name, Secondary Owners First and Last Name.
Output	•	Store owner name display

The first version is better because less data is being passed, while more of the processing (reading the store record) is being controlled by the subprogram. In the second example this read is outside of the subprogram, and is therefore harder to debug.

Chapter 13

Final Thoughts on Eliminating the GO TO

In this chapter we will present a more detailed discussion of GO TO processing, including our arguments against the use of GO TO EXIT processing. In his article "Go To Statement Considered Harmful" (Communications of the ACM, March 1968, P 147-148) Dr. Edsger W. Dijkstra observed that "The quality of a programmers work is a decreasing function of the density of GO TO statements in the programs they produce".

We can summarize his supporting arguments as follows. Once a program has been written, it becomes a process being executed on the computer. There is a point in the process that we must return to in order to repeat a portion of the process and have the same results. In other words "What data do we have to fix in order that we can redo the process until the very same point." This return to point is called the textual index. As the program becomes more complicated, and loops through more iterations, the programmer loses control of the value of the textual index. We can interpret the value of a variable only with respect the progress of the process from the textual index point. The GO TO statement makes it terribly hard to find a meaningful trace back to the textual index point, making it increasingly difficult to interpret the value of any given variable.

Thus the GO TO needs to be eliminated from our code because of the additional complications to the program that they create. The GO TO complicates the program by creating excessive labels in the program to give the GO TO a place to branch to, and by the creating multiple paths through the program process. We can see these two problems in the following example:

```
PRT-LP.
    ADD 1 TO PX1.
    IF PX1 > 13
        MOVE 'AL' TO WANT-ALL
        GO TO CHK-BYPASS.
    IF PRT-DST (PX1) NOT NUMERIC GO TO PRT-LP.
CHK-BYPASS.
    MOVE 1 TO PX1.
    IF BYPASS GO TO A4.
    OPEN INPUT PAYABLE-IN.
    MOVE 1 TO OLD-DATA-SW.
A1. READ PAYABLE-IN INTO PAY-OUT-1 AT END GO TO A2.
    ADD PO-COST TO IN-COST-CTL.
    PERFORM WRITE-INV-TAPE THRU TAPE-EXIT.
    GO TO A1.
A2. IF IN-COST-CTL = R-INV-CONTROL GO TO A3.
    IF RE-RUN
        GO TO A3.
    DISPLAY 'INVOICE TAPE CONTROL OUT OF BALANCE.
    MOVE 0002 TO ABCODE.
    GO TO DUMP-ROUT.
A3. CLOSE PAYABLE-IN.
    MOVE 0 TO OLD-DATA-SW.
A4.
    OPEN INPUT MERCHANDISE OUTPUT MDSE-OUT PRINTER.
    OPEN OUTPUT ESTMT-SALES.
    MOVE SPACES TO PRINT-OUT.
    OPEN I-O GROSS-OUT. MOVE 1 TO X1.
        MOVE 99999 TO G-P-IBM-DIST (X1).
B1. READ MERCHANDISE AT END GO TO CLOSE-FILES.
    MOVE SPACE TO SAVE-F.
```

B20.
    IF M-REPORT-CODE NOT NUMERIC
        MOVE 9 TO M-REPORT-CODE.
    IF CASH-BOOK
      IF M-MDSE-KEY = 150
        OR M-MDSE-KEY = 151
           GO TO B1
        ELSE GO TO PROCESS-CB.
B1A.

Here we see that the GO TOs cause the need for multiple labels which allow multiple paths though the program. Recoding this without the GO TOs and labels gives us the following piece of logic. As we can see this new version is much easier to understand than the original.

B000-PROCESS.
    PERFORM VARYING PX1 FROM 1 BY 1
                UNTIL PX1 > 13
    END-PERFORM.
    MOVE 'AL' TO WANT-ALL
    MOVE 1 TO PX1.
    IF BYPASS GO TO A4
      NEXT SENTENCE
    ELSE
      OPEN INPUT PAYABLE-IN.
      MOVE 1 TO OLD-DATA-SW.
      READ PAYABLE-IN AT END SET END-OF-PAYABLE-IN TRUE
      PERFORM UNTIL END-OF-PAYABLE-IN
         ADD PO-COST TO IN-COST-CTL.
         PERFORM WRITE-INV-TAPE THRU TAPE-EXIT
         READ PAYABLE-IN AT END SET END-OF-PAYABLE-IN TRUE
    END-PERFORM
    IF IN-COST-CTL = R-INV-CONTROL
    OR RE-RUN
      CLOSE PAYABLE-IN.
      MOVE 0 TO OLD-DATA-SW
    ELSE
      DISPLAY 'INVOICE TAPE CONTROL OUT OF BALANCE

```
          MOVE 0002 TO ABCODE
          GO TO DUMP-ROUT
      END-IF.

      OPEN INPUT MERCHANDISE  OUTPUT MDSE-OUT  PRINTER.
      OPEN OUTPUT ESTMT-SALES.
      MOVE SPACES TO PRINT-OUT.
      OPEN I-O GROSS-OUT.
      MOVE 1 TO X1.
      MOVE 99999 TO G-P-IBM-DIST (X1).
      READ MERCHANDISE  AT END  GO TO CLOSE-FILES.
      PERFORM UNTIL END-OF-MERCHANDISE
           MOVE SPACE TO SAVE-F
           IF M-REPORT-CODE NOT NUMERIC
              MOVE 9 TO M-REPORT-CODE
           END-IF
           IF CASH-BOOK AND M-MDSE-KEY = 150
           OR CASH-BOOK AND M-MDSE-KEY = 151
              CONTINUE
           ELSE
              GO TO PROCESS-CB
           END-IF
      END-PERFORM
      GO TO CLOSE-FILES.
```

The only valid exception to the "no GO TOs" rule is when the program executes an abend procedure, especially when the abend produces a core dump. This is true for two reasons. First, the distance between the textual index point where the abend occurred and the end of the process is the single GO TO ABEND command. Second, the process is ended and the values of the variables are set. If a corresponding core dump is produced, then the values of these variables are also thoroughly documented and can be easily reestablished.

However, some people feel that the use of the GO TO is still valid as long as you are only branching to the corresponding EXIT paragraph, using "GO TO EXIT" logic. The author has had a number of discussions

with people about the use of the "GO TO EXIT" method of programming. This is particularly true of one shop where it was required that every
paragraph have a corresponding exit paragraph.

In "GO TO EXIT" processing, the programmer checks for a certain
condition. If the condition is met, they bypass the rest of the processing of
that paragraph by branching to the corresponding exit paragraph instead
of executing the next instruction. Take the following code fragment for an
example:

```
A000-MAIN-PROCESS.
    PERFORM B100-PROCESS-INPUT
        THRU B100-PROCESS-INPUT-EXIT
        UNTIL 310-END-OF-FILE-FLAG = 'Y'.
    PERFORM E100-PGM-WRAPUP
        THRU E100-PGM-WRAPUP-EXIT.

B100-PROCESS-INPUT.
    PERFORM X100-READ-INPUT.
    IF 310-END-OF-FILE-FLAG = 'Y'
        GO TO B100-PROCESS-INPUT-EXIT.
    PERFORM B110-COMPUTE-COMMISSION
    .
    .
    PERFORM Y400-WRITE-RPT-LINE.

B100-PROCESS-INPUT-EXIT.
    EXIT.

X100-READ-INPUT.
    READ 100-INPUT-FILE INTO 910-INPUT-AREA
        AT END MOVE 'Y' TO 310-END-OF-FILE-FLAG.

    IF 310-END-OF-FILE-FLAG = 'N'
        ADD 1 TO 300-RECORDS-READ.
```

Here the paragraph B100-PROCESS-INPUT serves as the main repetitive drive paragraph of the program. After reading the input record, the

program checks the 310-END-OF-FILE-FLAG. If the end of file condition has been reached, the program jumps to the exit paragraph, which in turn exits the process, and ends the loop. The next statement to be executed will be the PERFORM E100-PGM-WRAPUP.

It is our contention that GO TO EXIT processing should not be used for the following reasons. First, that "GO TO EXIT" programming violates the rules of structured programming. Second, that the exit paragraph is redundant, and distracts from the readability of the program. And third, that the EXIT PARAGRAPH leads to poor coding habits.

Those who support GO TO EXIT PROCESSING have used the following arguments:

"Each paragraph in a program is a box, and the exit statement serves as the bottom of each box. Otherwise the top of the next box would serve as the bottom of this box. Having the exit serve as the bottom of the box makes the program more readable."

Instead of making the program more readable, the inclusion of the exit paragraph clutters the program for both the programmer and the compiler. This is because all we have actually done is insert an unnecessary "BOX" into the program.

We can see this by examining how the COBOL PERFORM verb functions. The COBOL PERFORM verb is actually a call to an internal subroutine.

In the example below we see a fragment of COBOL code, and the corresponding assembler code that the compiler built:

```
PERFORM B100-COMPUTE-COMMISSION.

B100-COMPUTE-COMMISSION.
    .
    .
    .

B100-COMPUTE-EXIT.
    EXIT.
```

```
            BAS  R14,COMPCOM   PERFORM B100-COMPUTE-COMMISSION
COMPCOM     EQU  *             B100-COMPUTE-COMMISSION
            ST   R14,COMPCOMR  SAVE RETURN ADDRESS
   .
   .
   .
            L    R14,COMPCOMR  GET RETURN ADDRESS
            BR   R14           BRANCH BACK
COMPCOMR DS      F             SAVE RETURN ADDRESS

COMPCOME EQU  *                B100-COMPUTE-EXIT
            L    R14,COMPCOMR  GET RETURN ADDRESS
            BR   R14           BRANCH BACK
```

The compiler translates the PERFORM COMMAND into the "BAS" (or branch and save the address) command, which also contains the label of the code to be executed. In this case the label is "COMPCOM". The performed paragraph "COMPCOM" then contains the following instructions:

1) Commands to save the address of where the paragraph was called from. Here we save the address in REGISTER 14, by executing the DS COMMAND (define storage) at address label "COMPCOMR".

2) The commands that do the paragraph's unit of work (which the author is too lazy to translate into assembler for this example).

3) The commands to return to the perform statement and then to continue the sequential processing. This consists of getting the address and then executing the BR (branch back).

The exit paragraph "COMPCOME" has the same commands as the last part of the performed paragraph.

This example allows us to make the following observations. First, instead of serving as the "bottom of a box", the exit paragraph is a separate entity, a separate box, with its own unique address and procedure code. Second, the exit paragraph is redundant, containing the same commands that allow the performed paragraph to return to the place from whence it came. Third, the exit paragraph adds unnecessary clutter to the compiled object module. It adds redundant instructions to the program, as well as unneeded entries to the symbol table. The effect of this duplication is increased dramatically when we remember that each paragraph in the program has a corresponding exit paragraph. And fourth, that the execution of the PERFORM THRU verb actually executes two subroutines (the paragraph to be performed, and the exit paragraph) whereas the simple perform statement executes a single subroutine.

When we call a subroutine we must know the address of the subroutine. In this case the address is "COMPCOM". We must also be able to tell the subroutine where the data is. In this case the data is in the working storage of the program. And we must be able to tell the subroutine how to branch back to the statement that started the process.

This allows us to define a subroutine as a portion of code with a specific address that is referenced by another portion of the program, independent access to all necessary data fields, and the ability to return to the place that invoked it.

Since the EXIT paragraph meets this definition, we must acknowledge that it is a subroutine. This means that using the PERFORM THRU verb to include a EXIT paragraph means we are calling two subroutines with the same command. This is especially true when there are additional paragraphs between the performed paragraph and the exit.

The exit paragraphs also make the program harder to read. Humans can only comprehend a finite number of concepts at a single time. By adding unnecessary exits to the program, we reduce the amount of "CORE MEMORY" that our reader has available for more important concepts.

The second argument is that "GO TO EXIT" processing does not violate the single exit rule of structured programming. If we add an "IF-GO TO EXIT" routine to our example, we will see how we then have multiple exits from our paragraph.

```
                BAS R14,COMPCOM   PERFORM B100-COMPUTE-COMMISSION
COMPCOM  EQU *                    B100-COMPUTE-COMMISSION
                ST  R14,COMPCOMR  SAVE RETURN ADDRESS
                CP  COMMAMT,0
                BZ  COMPCOME
       .
       .
       .
                L   R14,COMPCOMR  GET RETURN ADDRESS
                BR  R14           BRANCH BACK—B100
COMPCOMR DS  F                    SAVE RETURN ADDRESS

COMPCOME EQU *                    B100-COMPUTE-EXIT
                L   R14,COMPCOMR  GET RETURN ADDRESS
                BR  R14           BRANCH BACK—B100-EXIT
```

Here we have added instructions to check the value of "COMMANT" for zeroes. If "COMMANT" is equal to zeroes, then we will "GO TO EXIT" by branching to ("BZ") the label "COMPCOME". We will then execute the "BR" (BRANCH BACK) command with the comment "BRANCH BACK -B100-EXIT".

If "COMMANT" is not zero, then we will execute the unit of work of the paragraph, and then execute the "BR" command with the comment "BRANCH BACK—B100".

This means that paragraph B100-COMPUTE-COMMISSION actually has two exits, because there are two different ways to return to the calling paragraph. Thus "GO TO EXIT" processing violates the single entry-single exit rule.

The third argument is "That the exit paragraph is necessary so that you can branch around code, especially when trying to fix an abend."

If a program is properly structured, using the principles of coupling and cohesion, then there is nothing to branch around. If a paragraph is functionally cohesive, then all of the commands within that paragraph relate to the same function. If a new condition statement splits the functions, creating two independent functions, then the proper change is to split the paragraph into two separate paragraphs, and the IF statement should go into the drive paragraph.

For example, the code fragment

```
B100-MAIN-PROCESS.
    PERFORM B300-LOAD-REPORT-LINE.

B300-LOAD-REPORT-LINE.
    MOVE 910-INPUT-FIELD-1 TO 610-REPORT-FIELD-1.
    MOVE 910-INPUT-FIELD-2 TO 610-REPORT-FIELD-2.
    MOVE 910-INPUT-FIELD-3 TO 610-REPORT-FIELD-3.
    MOVE 910-INPUT-FIELD-4 TO 610-REPORT-FIELD-4.
    MOVE 910-INPUT-FIELD-5 TO 610-REPORT-FIELD-5.
    IF 910-INPUT-FIELD-6 = 'N'
        GO TO B300-EXIT.
    MOVE 910-INPUT-FIELD-6 TO 610-REPORT-FIELD-6.
    MOVE 910-INPUT-FIELD-7 TO 610-REPORT-FIELD-7.
    MOVE 910-INPUT-FIELD-8 TO 610-REPORT-FIELD-8.
    MOVE 910-INPUT-FIELD-9 TO 610-REPORT-FIELD-9.

B300-EXIT.
    EXIT.
```

Could easily have been written:

```
B100-MAIN-PROCESS.
    PERFORM B300-LOAD-BASE-RPT-LINE.
    IF 910-INPUT-FIELD-6 NOT EQUAL 'N'
        PERFORM B400-LOAD-EXTN-RPT-LINE.

B300-LOAD-REPORT-LINE.
    MOVE 910-INPUT-FIELD-1 TO 610-REPORT-FIELD-1.
```

```
      MOVE 910-INPUT-FIELD-2  TO  610-REPORT-FIELD-2.
      MOVE 910-INPUT-FIELD-3  TO  610-REPORT-FIELD-3.
      MOVE 910-INPUT-FIELD-4  TO  610-REPORT-FIELD-4.
      MOVE 910-INPUT-FIELD-5  TO  610-REPORT-FIELD-5.

B400-LOAD-EXTN-RPT-LINE.
      MOVE 910-INPUT-FIELD-6  TO  610-REPORT-FIELD-6.
      MOVE 910-INPUT-FIELD-7  TO  610-REPORT-FIELD-7.
      MOVE 910-INPUT-FIELD-8  TO  610-REPORT-FIELD-8.
      MOVE 910-INPUT-FIELD-9  TO  610-REPORT-FIELD-9.
```

This structure maintains the proper level of functional cohesion.

In sequentially cohesive modules, the need for a GO TO EXIT process is often caused by not initializing the loop. For example, instead of reading the input file at the top of PARAGRAPH B100-PROCESS-INPUT:

```
A000-MAIN-PROCESS.
      PERFORM B100-PROCESS-INPUT
          THRU B100-PROCESS-INPUT-EXIT
          UNTIL 310-END-OF-FILE-FLAG = 'Y'.
      PERFORM E100-PGM-WRAPUP
          THRU E100-PGM-WRAPUP-EXIT.

B100-PROCESS-INPUT.
      PERFORM X100-READ-INPUT.
      IF 310-END-OF-FILE-FLAG = 'Y'
          GO TO B100-PROCESS-INPUT-EXIT.
      PERFORM B110-COMPUTE-COMMISSION.
      .
      .
      PERFORM Y400-WRITE-RPT-LINE.

B100-PROCESS-INPUT-EXIT.
      EXIT.
```

We can do the initial read outside the loop, and the subsequent reads as the last step in our unit of work.

```
A000-MAIN-PROCESS.
    PERFORM X100-READ-INPUT.
    PERFORM B100-PROCESS-INPUT
        THRU B100-PROCESS-INPUT-EXIT
        UNTIL 310-END-OF-FILE-FLAG = 'Y'.
    PERFORM E100-PGM-WRAPUP
        THRU E100-PGM-WRAPUP-EXIT.

B100-PROCESS-INPUT.
    PERFORM B110-COMPUTE-COMMISSION
    .
    .
    PERFORM Y400-WRITE-RPT-LINE.
    PERFORM X100-READ-INPUT.
```

The perform until then takes care of the initial END-OF-FILE check, as well as the END-OF-FILE CHECK throughout the run. Doing this not only eliminates the GO TO EXIT, but we also eliminate the redundant END OF FILE CHECK.

GO TO EXITS in the other levels of cohesion can be eliminated by improving their level of cohesion. If there is something in the paragraph that you have to code around, then you have too many functions in the program.

The fourth argument is that "Go to exit is an acceptable coding method." When a technique reduces the level of structure of a paragraph, then it is not a proper technique. The use of the GO TO EXIT logic leads to quick fixes, to split paragraphs, and to ignoring of the rules of coupling and cohesion. Neatness counts, especially after you have to come along behind a sloppy programmer, and "unfix" everything that they did. And then one day I found an exit paragraph in a production program with forty lines of code in it, including an additional database call.

Thus we see that the use of the GO TO, including the GO TO EXIT process, should not be accepted.

Chapter 14

Conclusions

Throughout this text, we have been concerned with showing the principles of structured programming through the use of COBOL program fragments.

As we stated earlier, structured programming is the stepwise process of parsing program functions into a hierarchical chain of modules. Each of these modules perform a single task, are efficient and economical, contain the basic constructs of sequence, selection, and repetition, are free of GOTO processing, have a single entrance point, have a single exit point, have a minimum number of control statements, eliminate programming tricks, and are used to produce provable, reliable software systems.

As we have seen, this can be achieved by assembling programs from functionally cohesive modules that are executed by sequentially cohesive modules. These types of modules contain a single entry and a single exit point, and all of the process within the module is related.

Doing this allows us to use a single program structure for any application. This structure can be easily modified by simply adding, deleting, or changing modules as the business rules for the program change.

This modularization also allows us to separate the business rule modules from the data and presentation modules. This separation of modules allow us to simplify the maintenance process. A change to a data source only requires the data module to be changed. A change to a business rule only requires understanding of and changes to that module. This is turn leads to a reduction in the requirements for regression testing if an individual module is changed.

The use of functionally cohesive modules also eliminates the opportunity to use GO TO EXIT processing. Since all of the functionality within the module is related, there is nothing to branch around.

The use of sequentially cohesive modules eliminates the rest of the GO TO processing. Through proper structure and initialization of fields, the sequentially cohesive module can be executed without exception processing.

This modularity also allows us to improve the level of coupling between modules. As cohesion within the module is increased, the amount of control information that is passed between the modules is also reduced.

Modularity also allows us to improve the reliability of software systems, because we can reuse code from earlier programs that have already be proven to work. Testing then is a function of verifying that the already proven modules are executed in the proper order, and that they work together properly. These modules can be stored in copybook or other libraries. A change to a module in a copy library, and a recompile of its client programs, is mush easier than making individual changes to each program.

This modularity is achieved through the proper parsing of the program functions. Parsing is based on the concept of a unit of work. A unit of work consists of inputs, processes, rules that control the process, and resulting outputs. As we continue to parse a function, we will ultimately arrive at an elemental unit of work. An elemental unit of work has a single input, a single process, and a single output. We then build functional cohesive modules from each defined elemental unit of work. We then link these modules in sequentially cohesive modules, which control program execution.

Thus we can judge the structure of a program by the level of coupling and cohesion.

0-595-65034-1